CW00428253

StockpART

100 years of putting ART into Stockport

A Stockport Art Guild Publication celebrating its 2019 centenary

Written by Peter Davis MAFA

Cover images (from left to right):

1919	Watercolour of Beckfoot near Bingley by Walter Foster (Fig 6).
1924	'SSA 1924' Copper Tray made by Hugh Wallis for Walter Foster (Fig 7).
1925	Crowd for the 1925 opening of the War Memorial building (Fig 9).
1929	Clarence Northing sketching en plein air in 1929 (Fig 36).
1932	Hugh Wallis, co-founder of the Stockport Guild of Arts & Crafts (Fig 14).
1936	'Old Swanage, Dorset' by James Chettle (Fig 51).
1937	'September, Mottram' by Harry Rutherford (Fig 30).
1943	'Above the Valley' by James Chettle (Fig 62).
1947	John Davies sketching en plein air (Fig 66).
1950	The Mayor of Stockport viewing Stockport Art Guild's Annual Exhibition (Fig 74).
1972	June Bevan by John Chirnside (Fig 98).
1973	LS Lowry discussing exhibited works (Fig 88).
1973	'Car Park' by Hal Yates (Fig 95).
1979	Self-portrait by John Chirnside (Fig 104).
1985	Glass engraving "Underbank Hall Stockport" by Carole Dronsfield (Fig 123).
1995	A painting of Stockport College by June Bevan (Fig 82).
2000	'Jimmy and Toots' by Mike Heath (Fig 109).
2005	Christopher Rose-Innes at work in his studio (Fig 122).
2008	'Shops and Bollards (Stockport)' by John Dronsfield (Fig 115).
2013	'Aunty Winnie' by Angela Herd Hall (Fig 118).
2017	'Cardboard Reality 1' by Peter Davis (Fig 147).
2018	'The Birling Gap' by Ron Coleman (Fig 117).
2019	Peter Davis (left) with Dave Foster (right), grandson of Walter Foster (Fig 151).

First edition. Published in 2019 by Stockport Art Guild
www.stockportartguild.com

Peter Davis asserts the moral right to be identified as the author of this work.

Every effort has been made by the author and the publisher to seek permission to reproduce the images in this book whose copyright does not reside with Stockport Art Guild, and we are grateful to the individuals and institutions who have assisted us with this task. Images for which no source is given come from the Stockport Art Guild Archives. Apologies for any errors or omissions that may inadvertently have occurred and we will be pleased to make the necessary corrections in any future edition.

All rights reserved. No part of this publication may be reproduced, distributed, or transmitted in any form or by any means, including photocopying, recording, or other electronic or mechanical methods, without the prior written permission of the publisher, except in the case of brief quotations embodied in critical reviews and certain other non-commercial uses permitted by copyright law.

© 2019 Stockport Art Guild
Reg. No. 1069 S&L Register of Friendly Societies
ISBN no 978-1-5272-3343-0

Contents

Foreword

This year, 2019, the Stockport Art Guild is one hundred years old and The Guild`s Council felt that the centenary should be commemorated by a published history of the Guild. Peter Davis, a Council member, bravely volunteered to research and write this.

Readers of this book cannot fail to be impressed by the detail in this account covering 100 years of the Stockport Art Guild, even more so when one learns that there was no organised Guild archive for the author to consult. The compilation of this history involved months searching through more or less random documents and records as well as interviewing numerous people involved with the Guild over many years.

The result is not just a history of the Stockport Art Guild but also reveals trends and conflicts occurring in the wider art world: craft versus art; abstraction versus representation etc. The Guild IS the artists who belong to it, and the vignettes throughout the book of Guild members, artistically distinguished and otherwise, bring the whole account to life. This volume is a fitting celebration of the centenary of the Stockport Art Guild, which survived and operated uninterrupted though two world wars. Peter Davis is to be congratulated on producing it.

Christopher Rose-Innes MRSS
President, Stockport Art Guild, 2019

Introduction

This book has been written to mark a very important milestone: the 2019 Centenary of Stockport Art Guild. It is a society whose roots are firmly planted in the nineteenth century principles of the Arts and Crafts Movement but, with the help of some of the North West's most notable artists, it has evolved through the last century to become a modern and diverse art society now thriving in the twenty-first century.

I would like to take this opportunity to thank all the people who have helped me track down all the missing information, pointed me in the right direction and assisted me with local interviews. Writing this book has been both a labour of love and an onerous responsibility. At times it has felt like I've been putting back together a 10,000-piece jigsaw whilst blindfolded and when most of the pieces are missing. Until the start of this centennial project, Stockport Art Guild has not had an archivist and so, apart from a sporadic pile of old Guild Council minutes and exhibition catalogues, there were no neatly compiled records, newspaper articles or photographs that we could draw upon.

Stepping into the shoes of Stockport Guild's forefathers has given me a newfound respect for the society. I feel I have relived all the trials and tribulations, in addition to the compliments and condemnations, of the past hundred years and I look forward to sharing them with you.

I have endeavoured to tell the true history of Stockport Art Guild. I have chosen to do this chronologically, except when I delve into the individual lives of some of SAG's most notable past and current members. I apologise in advance if you feel any information, anecdotes or events are inadvertently incorrect or have been omitted - or if any members past or present feel they have been overlooked - please be assured this was not intentional.

The last thing I would like to add before embarking on this journey of how the Guild put ART into Stockport is that I hope this book will give readers a sense of what an amazing period the past one hundred years has been for the Stockport Guild and for the development of art in the town. It would be a wonderful legacy if it also helps to inspire the next generation of local artists.

Peter Davis MAFA
Archivist, Stockport Art Guild, 2019

To Lisa and Tony

Many thanks.

Peter

1910s

How It All Began

Fig 1 (detail): Walter Foster, self-portrait (circa 1908). Inaugural President of the Stockport Guild of Arts & Crafts.

Reaction to Industrialisation

Before embarking on a description of the formation of the society now known as Stockport Art Guild, it is important to delve a bit further back into the second half of the nineteenth century to get a sense of the industrial and social changes that were happening at that time.

By the middle of the nineteenth century, Manchester was Britain's second city and, thanks to its booming cotton industry, was becoming known as the 'workshop of the world.' Mill owners had invested heavily in modern machinery. However, the shift to using mechanical power as a substitute for muscle power was starting to be questioned by certain sections within society.

The Arts and Crafts Movement

In 1861, William Morris, Peter Marshall and Charles Faulkner formed a radical new decorative arts company called Morris, Marshall, Faulkner & Co. This was in response to The Industrial Revolution and the 'rise of the machines' that was rapidly changing the landscape, both around the mill towns of the North and culturally at the time. The company's primary aim was to make beautiful and simple handcrafted designs that would divert people away from the poor quality, industrially made products that were becoming the norm.

Although Morris & Co never fully realised their utopian Arts and Craft dream to create a society rooted in art, craftsmanship and quality of life, they inspired John Ruskin, another passionate social reformer and anti-industrialist who, in 1871, established the Guild of St. George.

The next decade saw Charles Ashbee, William Lethaby and William Benson, amongst others, lead the creative movement that took hold throughout the country and saw the emergence of dozens of Guilds under the banner of 'Arts and Crafts'. By the end of the 1880s the Arts and Crafts Exhibition Society, led by book illustrator Walter Crane, was working hard to make decorative arts as respectable as fine art.

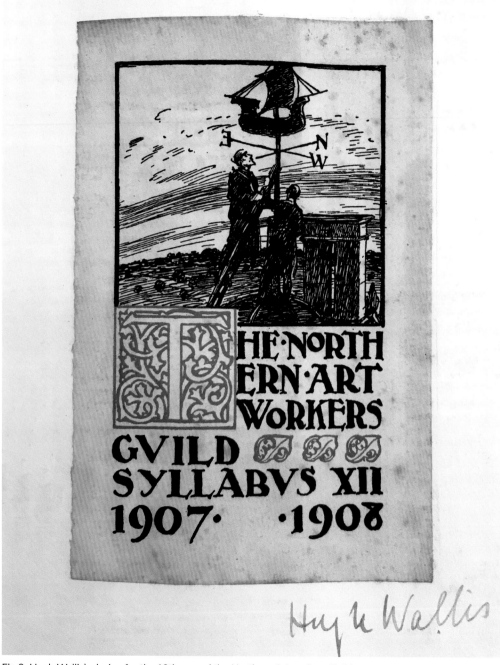

Fig 2: Hugh Wallis's design for the 12th year of the Northern Artworkers Guild.

For the next fifteen years, the Arts and Crafts Movement (ACM) flourished in Britain and by the beginning of the twentieth century over 130 Associations and Guilds of Arts and Crafts had sprung up in cities like Glasgow, London and Manchester. Although these groups were made up of diverse, multi-disciplinary professions such as metalworkers, sculptors, potters, stained glass makers, architects, designers and fine artists, the ACM believed it was paramount that all the skill sets were considered equally important and no art or craft was regarded as superior to any other.

Unity in the Arts

In 1896, Edgar Wood formed the Northern Art Workers' Guild with the help of Walter Crane who was Director of Design at the Manchester School of Art. In keeping with the principles of the ACM, its motto was 'Unity in the Arts.' By the turn of the century, the Northern Art Workers' Guild was amongst the most active and successful of the provincial Guilds. Another designer and craftsman by the name of Hugh Wallis played a key part in this group and was their honorary secretary from 1901 to 1905 and then their Master of the Guild in 1907. Wallis exhibited metalware, wallpaper designs, illustrations and paintings in their exhibitions at the Municipal School of Technology and Manchester Art Gallery. The last exhibition that the Northern Art Workers' Guild held was in the spring of 1911. Thereafter, the group went into decline and disappeared without trace.

The Arts and Crafts Movement continued to be the principal force in British art until the beginning of the First World War. However, by the end of the war the country had changed and the fear of industrialisation had passed and people were looking for the next creative crusade. The Arts and Crafts movement went into decline.

Changes afoot on Greek Street

Back in Stockport, by 1912 there were over one hundred and seventy children at Stockport Grammar School, known as 'The Old Grammar School.' The small school building on Greek Street, which was built in 1830 in the style of Tudor Gothic, was now overcrowded. As there was no room to extend satisfactorily on the site, the decision was made that the school would move.

Stockport Grammar School moved from Greek Street to their current site on Buxton Road in 1915 and shortly after hired a well-respected local artist and teacher called Walter Potts who taught art at the school until his retirement in 1948.

An idea to build an Art Gallery in the town had started to gather momentum amongst a consortium of local Stockport councillors and industrialists. It was felt that Stopfordians (a demonym for the people of Stockport), had great potential but no opportunity to experience important things like art, technology and culture.

Fig 3: 'The Old Grammar School' on Greek Street – view from Wellington Road (circa 1910).

In 1915, the Greek Street site was sold to Mr. Samuel Kay JP for £5,000 and the building was used for a few years as another school, an evening college and a hall for hire. At a public meeting on the 19th September 1919, the consortium's idea took a big step closer to reality when it was decided that a spectacular War Memorial & Art Gallery would be built on the site of the Greek Street School in memory of the men who had died in the Great War.

At the end of the conflict, towns and villages throughout the country were building their own memorials to remember the dead. The Great War had taken the lives of so many Stopfordians that the town felt something had to be done to mark their sacrifice.

Fig 4: The Greek Street School in May 1921, shortly before the site was cleared to make way for the War Memorial building.

COUNTY BOROUGH OF STOCKPORT.

WAR MEMORIAL FUND.

Chairman of Committee :

THE MAYOR OF STOCKPORT (ALDERMAN CHARLES ROYLE).

Chairman of Executive Committee :

CAPTAIN G. CHRISTIE-MILLER, D.S.O., M.C.

Hon. Secretaries :   *General Secretary :*

MR. F. CONNELL, J.P.   MR. JAMES BELL, B.A.
MR. WM. ASTLE, J.P.

Hon. Treasurer :

LT.-COLONEL W. CHALONER, T.D.

Executive Committee :

MR. JOHN ATKINSON.	MR. W. JOHNSTON, J.P.	MRS. T. W. POTTS.
COUNCR. HENRY BELL, D.L.	MR. JAMES LOMAS.	REV. CANON ROCHE.
MRS. N. BENNETT.	MR. MALBON.	COUNCR. T. ROWBOTHAM, J.P.
MR. C. R. BRADY.	MR. MOORE.	MISS ROWBOTHAM. M.A.
ALDERMAN HENRY GREEN.	DR. R. A. MURRAY, J.P.	MR. H. SPARES.
COUNCR. J. GREENHALGH.	MR. P. PEIRCE, J.P.	MR. W. G. WARD, J.P.
MR. ROBERT HYDE.	COUNCR. T. W. POTTS, O.B.E.	

MAYOR'S PARLOUR,
STOCKPORT.
December, 1919.

THE EXECUTIVE COMMITTEE appointed to carry into effect the resolution of the General Committee to erect on the Site of the Old Grammar School a building which shall fitly perpetuate the memory of the Stockport men who laid down their lives in the Great War, now appeal to their fellow-citizens for the financial support to enable them to execute the work.

Careful consideration was given to all the schemes submitted in reply to the request for suggestions made through the local Press, and having regard to the desirability of placing the memorial in a central position easily accessible to all the inhabitants, the Old Grammar School site was found to be the one most generally approved.

Fig 5: The fundraising appeal, launched by the War Memorial Committee in December 1919.

Within a few months, the trustees of the late Samuel Kay donated the site on which the school building stood to the Corporation of Stockport, and the building was demolished to make way for the new War Memorial & Art Gallery.

It was agreed that the War Memorial building should have three elements:
- a commemorative sculpture
- a memorial hall
- an exhibition gallery.

A committee was formed to oversee the design and construction of the War Memorial Building by Manchester architects Halliday and Agate. The founding chairmen were Alderman Charles Royle JP and Captain G Christie-Miller. Other members at the time included: Lt Colonel W Chaloner, Councillor Henry Bell, Councillor J Greenhalgh and Councillor TW Potts OBE.

By the end of the War, the national debt was equivalent to 136% of the country's gross national product (GDP). Stockport, in common with the majority of borough councils, could barely fund the rebuilding of the towns after the bombings, let alone fund a project like the Stockport War Memorial. As a result, the committee took the decision that the new building had to be paid for by public subscription. Stopfordians clearly felt they needed a memorial to act as a focus for their grief and remembrance and the response to the public fundraising appeal from ordinary people, tradesmen and benefactors was magnificent. The finance was raised and the building, once completed in 1925, was donated to the Town Council, free of debt.

Foundation of the Stockport Guild of Arts & Crafts (SGAC)

In 1919, a small group of like-minded Stockport artists and craftsmen began meeting in each other's homes to participate in creative practices and discuss their shared passion for the Arts and Crafts Movement. Amongst the initial group of founding members were: Frederick Davenport Bates, Harry Garner, Walter Kirkman, Joseph Knowles, Walter Potts, Annie Storey and Hugh Wallis. The gatherings quickly gained members and soon a constitution had been written and agreed and the Stockport Guild of Arts & Crafts had begun.

Fig 1: Walter Foster, self-portrait (circa 1908). Inaugural President of the Stockport Guild of Arts & Crafts.

Walter Foster

In 1921, Walter Foster was elected the first President of the Stockport Guild of Arts & Crafts.

Foster was born in 1887 and attended the junior school of Bingley Grammar School. By the age of twelve, his innate artistic talent had been spotted by the art master at the Bingley School of Art who offered him a job as his assistant.

Four years later, when he was just sixteen, he won a scholarship to the Royal College of Art (RCA) and became one of their youngest ever students. He studied there from 1903-1908, developing his skills in painting, sculpture, architecture, stained glass design and woodcarving. During this period, the Arts and Crafts Movement's leading exponents were running the College.

After gaining a full Diploma and an Associateship (ARCA), Foster returned to Yorkshire where he taught art at Halifax Secondary School, Bingley School of Art and Bingley Grammar School. In 1915, he enlisted as a volunteer in the Royal Navy during the First World War. After the conflict he returned to Yorkshire and from April 1920 to March 1921 he worked at Lister's Mills in Bradford studying textile colouration and design, before relocating across the Pennines to Stockport to become Headmaster at the Stockport School of Art on Wellington Road. Annie Storey, John Sandiford and Harry Garner, members of the SGAC, were all on the teaching staff at the Stockport School of Art when Foster joined the school.

Fig 6: Watercolour of Beckfoot near Bingley by Walter Foster (1919)

Fig 7: Detail of Copper Tray made by Hugh Wallis for Walter Foster.

Foster's career drew him back to Yorkshire in 1924 where he became Headmaster at Shipley School of Art. His leaving gift from Stockport School of Art (SSA) was a tray designed and made by his good friend and fellow SGAC member, Hugh Wallis.

Walter Foster was Stockport Guild's President from 1921-24. During his tenure, he saw more and more members join, meetings become more formalised and the society's aims grow more ambitious. In addition to being the headmaster of the Stockport Art School, he was also a Freemason and so the Guild began using the local Masonic Meeting Hall on Greek Street for exhibitions and the Art School for their weekly painting sessions and Council meetings. Unbeknownst to Walter Foster and the other founders, they had laid the foundations for what would become one of the most enduring and important arts societies in the North West.

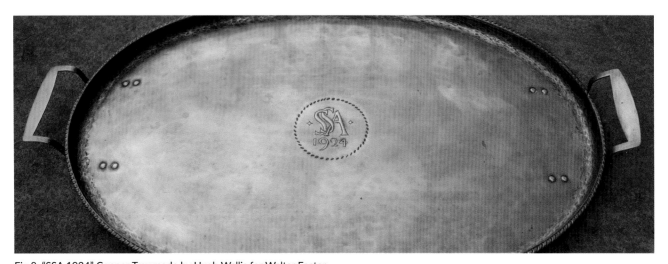

Fig 8: "SSA 1924" Copper Tray made by Hugh Wallis for Walter Foster.

1920s

A Strong and Lusty Sapling

Fig 9: Crowd for the 1925 opening of the War Memorial building.

Hugh Wallis

Born in 1871, Hugh Wallis was one of nine children in an artistic and nature-loving Quaker family. At the age of 20 he moved to Bushey in Hertfordshire for three years to study art at the innovative Herkomer Art School. It is a measure of his artistic ability that, in 1893, he was awarded the Herkomer Scholarship, entitling him to free tuition there.

After qualifying from Herkomer, Wallis began his career as a professional artist, primarily painting, drawing and doing design work. He began metalworking as a hobby but it soon proved to be so profitable that he decided to make it the focus of his profession. By the turn of the century he had moved to Altrincham and within a few years had begun his own metalworking business employing 5 or 6 craftsmen at his home and studio at 72 The Downs. The Arts and Crafts style was a major influence on his designwork.

Hugh Wallis continued to support and exhibit with the SGAC throughout the twenties and thirties. However, by 1921, when the SGAC was just two and a half years old, he was lured away to become the co-founder of another new Guild based in Lancaster, The Red Rose Guild of Artworkers. Its other co-founder, Margaret Pilkington, was closely associated with the Arts and Crafts Movement in Manchester and London and was determined only to accept artists and craftsmen of the highest standard, which attracted Wallis. Over the next few decades, membership of the Red Rose Guild grew rapidly

Fig 10: Promotional design by Hugh Wallis.

Fig 11: Promotional design by Hugh Wallis.

Fig 12: 'On the road to fairyland' oil on canvas by Hugh Wallis (circa 1904).

and it became one of the most highly regarded and influential Arts and Crafts Guilds in the country. Hugh Wallis served on their Executive Committee as Vice-Chairman and Chairman for sixteen years from 1921 to 1937.

Wallis was actively involved in the artistic life of the community, through exhibitions of his work and the contribution he made to the societies and associations of which he was a member, such as the Northern Art Workers' Guild, the Stockport Guild of Arts & Crafts, the Red Rose Guild and the Manchester Academy of Fine Arts. Hugh Wallis continued working until his death on the 13th December 1943, aged 72 years.

Fig 13: 'Three members by another' by Hugh Wallis. Exhibited in the Royal Academy in 1919.

Fig 14: Hugh Wallis, co-founder of the Stockport Guild of Arts & Crafts (circa 1932).

Fig 15: Handmade Metalwork by Hugh Wallis.

The Consecration of an Ideal

In 1922, at Stockport Guild's second Annual General Meeting at the Masonic Hall in Greek Street, President Foster, stood up and made a speech:

"I much appreciate the honour of presiding at this the 2nd annual meeting of the Stockport Guild of Arts & Crafts. From the small acorn grows a strong and sturdy oak, and there cannot be any doubt that our particular seed has germinated and is growing into a strong and lusty sapling. We are stronger numerically than we were a year ago, and one of the most encouraging signs is that we have received applications for membership from outside districts.

As the Mayor pointed out in his speech at the opening of our recent exhibition, the influence of our Guild in a purely industrial town cannot but be productive of much good. The variety of the work exhibited at that Exhibition was a great advance on the first year. Especially pleasing were the many exhibits of applied art as distinct from decorative art. The bold step that we made this year in holding the Annual Exhibition in an independent building fully justified itself, and we feel sure that the increased interest and publicity obtained, more than compensated for the extra costs involved.

I would like to take this opportunity of urging all members who are present to endeavour by all means to promote the interest of the Guild. It needs sacrifice for the consecration of an ideal and I feel sure that the ideas of this Guild are worthy of very great sacrifice. The Council would like to feel that they simply act as your executive and not to supply the enthusiasm that should emanate from every member and student member. Time does not permit any review of our past year's work, and our members will be familiar with most of the details. Suffice to say, that we have reason to be pleased with the leavening influence of our activities and the success that we have already achieved should encourage us to still further efforts on behalf of the ideals of the Stockport Guild of Arts & Crafts."

In November that year, the Stockport Guild exhibition of 1922 ran for just four days at the Masonic Hall. The Mayor, Alderman Charles Royle JP opened the exhibition and said:

> "While we have some ugly places in the town, there are some beautiful, and it is often only through seeing the ugly that we realise the presence of the beautiful. We have in the Guild of Arts and Crafts a band of ladies and gentlemen who are intent on transforming the ugly into the beautiful, and some day, though not perhaps in their time, the ugly spots of Stockport will be transformed."

He said he was glad, as a member of the Education Committee, that there was an awakening of a sense of the beautiful. He went on to say:

> "On that road (Greek Street) the old Grammar School is being taken down, and in its place there is to be erected the town's War Memorial. It is going to be a beautiful building and, when the Secondary School is extended, it will be connected with the Art School."

The Stockport Advertiser reported that:

> "There is much that lovers of the beautiful can admire that Stockportonians [sic] can regard with satisfaction and pride, in the Annual Exhibition, promoted by the Stockport Guild of Arts & Crafts. The Guild is comparatively a young institution, but it is very active and essentially progressive. Its members realise that both beauty and art take many forms and are to be expressed not only in pictures, but in articles made of various materials."

The Manchester Guardian also wrote about the exhibition that year, describing the Stockport art scene at the time:

> "Too many local art societies have confined their activities to the production of pictures of a more or less amateur kind. The Stockport Guild has taken a wider view, realizing that art is concerned with ordinary things for use and ornament as well as landscapes or portraits. The wholesale application of machinery to the production of furniture, jewellery, and almost everything else has indeed

a kind of temporary insanity from which the world is slowly recovering. Partly through the splendid but not quite effective protest of William Morris, people are beginning to attempt a more exact delimitation of the place of machine work and the place of handwork in industry and art. Where exactness and uniformity of certain kinds are chiefly needed, the machine is invaluable; where variation and the neo-expression of individuality are required, and in things of considerable intrinsic value, handwork will always hold its place."

The journalist went on:

"Some of the work at the Stockport Guild exhibition is of this educational kind, rather experimental than final. Work like that in metal by Mr Hugh Wallis is, of course, done with very professional skill, and various stages between are illustrated in other exhibits. An interesting approach to a healthy relationship between art and craftsmanship is suggested by the fact that two of the contributors who send fresh watercolour landscapes to the exhibition are in their ordinary practice professional decorators. Others, besides Mr Harry Garner and Mr Joseph Knowles, who show vigorous work in the pictoral section are Mr Cronshaw, Mr J. Lees Robinson, Mr H Tattersall and the President of the Guild, Mr WC Foster."

Walter Foster, Hugh Wallis, Walter Potts and Harry Rutherford all had a number of paintings on display. Mr J.H. Cronshaw ARCA, Master of the Heginbottom School of Art in Ashton-under-Lyne, submitted four paintings that he had produced of the town of Bruges. Frederick 'Davenport' Bates was also well-represented with several oil paintings, including a couple entitled 'Harvest' and 'Moonrise'. He also had a small, but skilfully executed portrait study on show. Several prizes were awarded that year: RH Kershaw won the Crafts section; the General Art, Elementary section, went to AP Chadwick and the Advanced section was awarded to James Bannister. In special prizes, the best sketches done on a Guild excursion went to Miss G Cooke; best lettering was awarded to Frank Brown; best example of stencilling was given to Anne Nuttall and Poster design was awarded to AP Chadwick.

A letter written around 1923 by Anne Nuttall on behalf of the Guild Council discusses how Stockport Guild's growing number of members could be brought closer in touch with each other. In it, she explains that Walter Foster has been granted special permission to create:

> *"...a special life class which can be held in the life room of the Art School and to which only full members of the Guild would be admitted.*
>
> *Guild Members desirous of associating themselves with this movement would be required to pay a fee to the School Govenors of 7/6 and in addition to subscribe to the cost of the model for posing. Members subscribing to this evening would be expected to subscribe to the Model's fee whether attending or not."*

On 8th March 1923, Walter Foster demonstrated his innate leadership skills with a rousing opening speech at the Stockport Guild's third AGM:

> *"We are not only stronger in numbers as a Guild than we were last year but our work is stronger – it is upon a higher plane. We must not be satisfied to remain where we are but continue to strive to higher things. Although some of us are fully-fledged members, we are still students in the strictest sense of the word. When we are satisfied with our work it necessarily follows we are on the downward path.*
>
> *We must continually aim at the encouragement of the 'fine arts and crafts', whoever has an interest in their pursuits in Stockport, must somehow be persuaded to join our Guild because the stronger we are, the more power we possess. We must not glory in exhibiting our work too much, but rather, exhibit with the intention of helping others.*
>
> *A step in the right direction has been made by forming a 'Guild Night', where full members meet once per week for study and for discussion of art matters in general. Let us make these meetings a huge success, perhaps it needs a certain amount of sacrifice to attend, but it is only by sacrifice we get on to the road of success.*

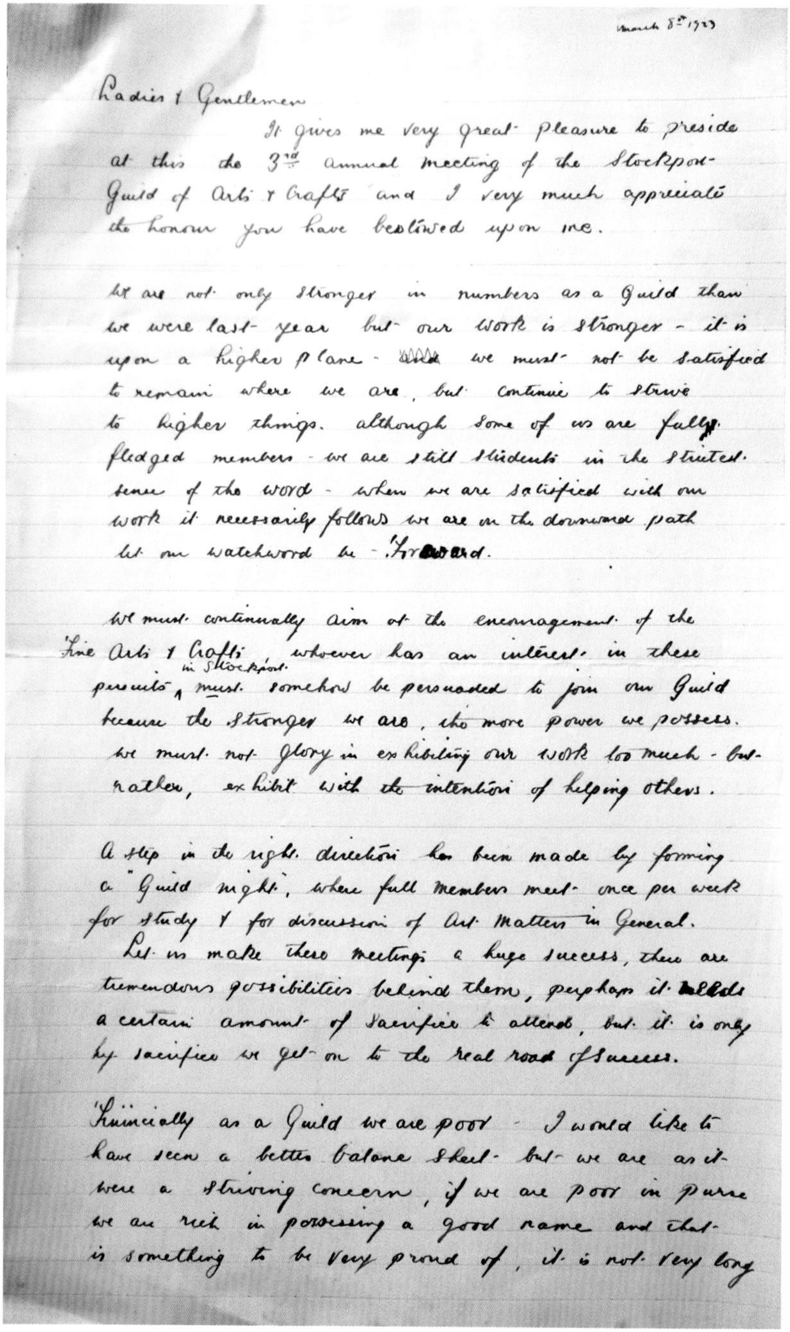

March 8th 1923

Ladies & Gentlemen

It gives me very great pleasure to preside at this the 3rd annual meeting of the Stockport Guild of Arts & Crafts and I very much appreciate the honour you have bestowed upon me.

We are not only stronger in numbers as a Guild than we were last year but our work is stronger - it is upon a higher plane - we must not be satisfied to remain where we are, but continue to strive to higher things. although some of us are fully fledged members - we are still students in the strictest sense of the word - when we are satisfied with our work it necessarily follows we are on the downward path let our watchword be - "Forward".

We must continually aim at the encouragement of the Fine Arts & Crafts in Stockport, whoever has an interest in these pursuits, must somehow be persuaded to join our Guild because the stronger we are, the more power we possess. we must not glory in exhibiting our work too much - but rather, exhibit with the intention of helping others.

A step in the right direction has been made by forming a "Guild night", where full members meet once per week for study & for discussion of Art Matters in General. Let us make these meetings a huge success, there are tremendous possibilities behind them, perhaps it entails a certain amount of sacrifice to attend, but it is only by sacrifice we get on to the real road of success.

Financially as a Guild we are poor - I would like to have seen a better balance sheet but we are as it were a striving concern, if we are poor in purse we are rich in possessing a good name and that is something to be very proud of, it is not very long

Fig 16: Walter Foster's handwritten speech for the Stockport Guild's 3rd AGM on 8th March 1923.

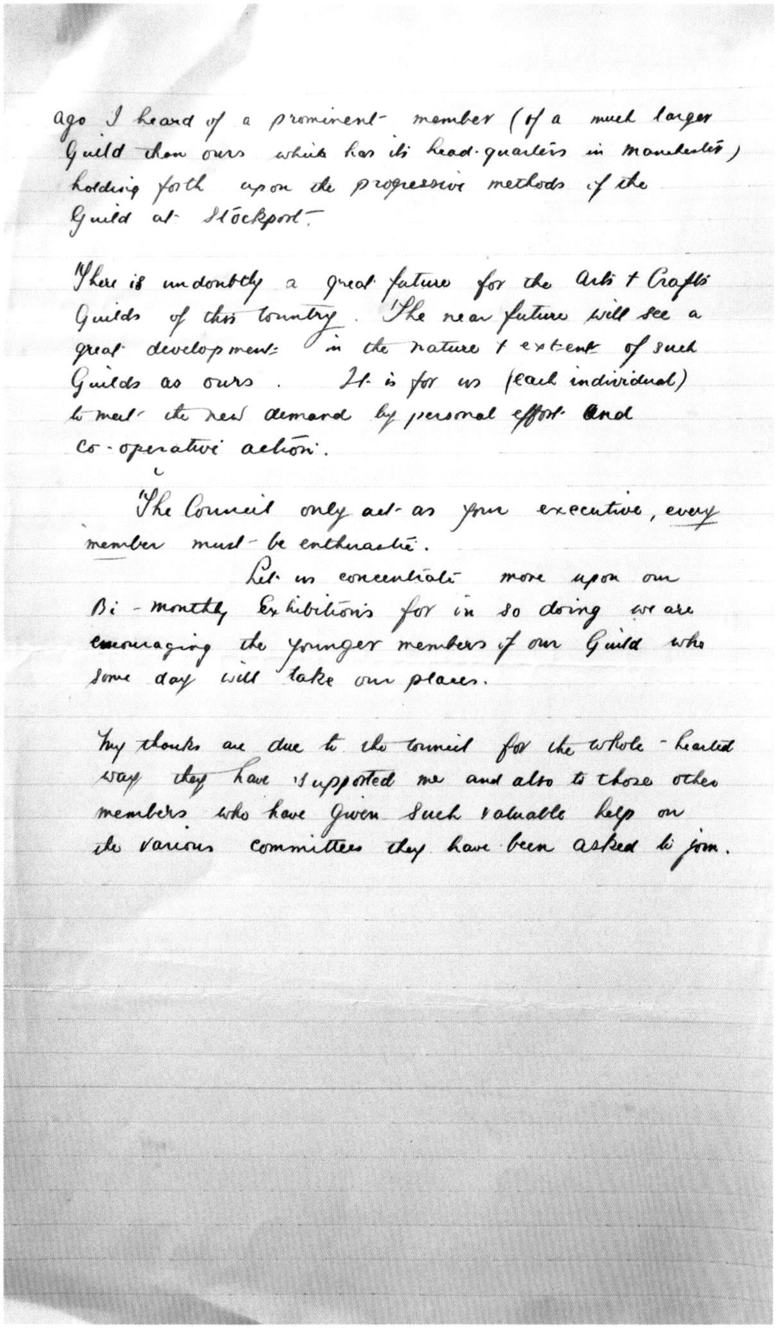

ago I heard of a prominent member (of a much larger Guild than ours which has its head-quarters in Manchester) holding forth upon the progressive methods of the Guild at Stockport.

There is undoubtly a great future for the Arts & Crafts Guilds of this Country. The near future will see a great development in the nature & extent of such Guilds as ours. It is for us (each individual) to meet the new demand by personal effort and co-operative action.

The Council only act as your executive, every member must be enthusiastic.

Let us concentrate more upon our Bi-monthly Exhibitions for in so doing we are encouraging the younger members of our Guild who some day will take our places.

My thanks are due to the Council for the whole-hearted way they have supported me and also to those other members who have given such valuable help on the various committees they have been asked to join.

Fig 17: Walter Foster's handwritten speech for the Stockport Guild's 3rd AGM on 8th March 1923.

'Financially' as a Guild we are poor – I would like to have seen a better balance sheet, but we are as it were a striving concern. If we are poor in purse we are rich in possessing a good name and that is something to be very proud of. It is not very long ago I heard a prominent member (of a much larger Guild than ours which has its headquarters in Manchester) holding forth upon the progressive methods of the Guild at Stockport.

There is undoubtedly a great future for the Arts and Crafts Guilds of this country. The near future will see a great development in the nature and extent of such Guilds as ours. It is for us (each individual) to meet the new demand by personal effort and co-operative action."

In November 1923, the society held its Annual Exhibition in the Masonic Hall, once again for just four days. The Manchester Guardian reported on it, saying that:

"...members are trying to both increase the scope and raise the standard of the exhibition. Handicraft is in itself a good thing to encourage. The Stockport Guild show a good deal of fairly elementary craftwork and other work in wood, leather, jewellery and metal that is of a much more professional character and shows much more careful thought both in design and workmanship. Two outside exhibits, respectively of metalwork and of handwoven stuffs, are a very useful feature in the show, which also includes a good number of pictures in oil and watercolour that are fresh and vigorous. A public Art Gallery is now being built in Stockport, but, in the meantime, the Arts Guild has done a good deal to indicate one direction in which it may be useful."

The Stockport Advertiser reviewed the show from a brutally honest local perspective, declaring that the exhibition showed:

"That Stockport is not the sordid, inartistic place that some people imagine it to be. One aim (of the Guild) is to get young members as students, so that their work can be compared with other work more mature, and thus they can get an idea of their capabilities. The society is also keen on helping and developing

crafts, especially those in which ex-servicemen are concerned. It also aims at combining local Guilds, which are to be found all over the country, into a national movement, and so be able to hold one big national exhibition."

The newspaper went on to reveal the fragility of the local group's existence:

"It may be stated that the Stockport Guild has been a struggle, but it has been self-supporting, having been run by the subscriptions and help of the members themselves. The society is entitled to ask for public sympathy and support, for it is undoubtedly doing a valuable work. The fact is that a lot of the trouble in life is due to the inability of people to see the beauty that is about them."

Aside from the work of Hugh Wallis, there were some noteworthy exhibits in the craft section that year. The Stockport Advertiser stated:

"The furniture and craftwork by Mr WE Carrington JP, and Mr JW Simpson, are interesting for more than one reason. The design is chaste, the execution is first-class, and the wood used has an historical interest, having been taken from old buildings now demolished, in one case the timber being over 600 years old."

One of the most striking pictures on display that year was 'Portrait of a Pianist', full of character and life, painted by Harry Rutherford. Walter Foster had an oil painting called 'Early Morning in September' and a watercolour entitled

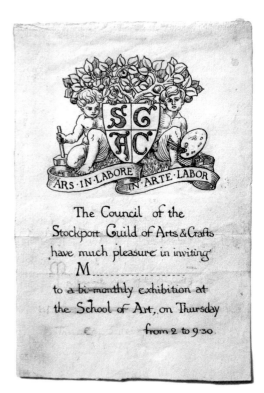

Fig 18: Walter Foster's hand-drawn Stockport Guild of Arts & Crafts invitation for bi-monthly exhibitions, circa 1923.

'Edge of the Moors' on show. William Shone submitted a couple of landscapes and a furniture design sketch. And last but not least, an artist by the name of Tom Scott, who had joined the Guild that year, exhibited a number of etchings and watercolour drawings - the most noteworthy of which was said to have been 'Valenciennes after the Armistice, 1918.' Little did he know that, in years to come, Scott would become one of the Guild's most important figures.

The War Memorial Building Opens

The War Memorial building was completed in the autumn of 1925. The final cost came in at £24,000, the whole of which was raised by voluntary subscriptions from all sections of the public of Stockport, which is incredible considering that post war unemployment by this time had reached its highest point (11.3%) since records began.

Fig 19: Official postcard, produced for the 1925 opening of the War Memorial building by HRH Prince Henry.

Fig 9: Crowd for the 1925 opening of the War Memorial building.

There was a huge, emotional turnout for the opening of the building by HRH Prince Henry on the 15th October 1925 - the streets were packed as all the Stopfordians who had funded it came to celebrate its opening. Society was now undoubtedly more democratic than it had ever been and the events of the early 1920s felt like an important milestone on the road to a more modern Britain.

Shortly after the building had been completed and unveiled it was handed over to the Education Committee of the Municipal Council free from debt. The majority of the individuals that had served on the War Memorial Build Committee transferred across to a War Memorial Gallery Committee that sat within a wider Education Committee at the Municipal Council. These included, Alderman Greenhalgh, Lieutenant Colonel Christie-Miller and a local businessman by the name of Mr James Chettle.

Fig 20: James Chettle.

James Chettle

A keen amateur artist, James Chettle (1871-1944), made his fortune as a successful cotton trader, running his own textile wholesale business in Manchester called JP Chettle Ltd. Although he was so closely connected with business, throughout his life he devoted his leisure time to painting.

"I liked painting at school, and I think showed ability in it, but afterwards for 20 years I was busy building up my business and never touched a brush. Then on holidays, I would occasionally do a sketch, but I was 42 before I began to take it seriously." He mainly painted landscapes in oil or watercolour, with the uplands of Derbyshire and the lowlands of East Anglia as his favourite subjects.

In the early 1920s Chettle relocated from Manchester to Davenport, initially living in 'Wythburn', Davenport Park Road, before moving onto 'The Cottage' in nearby Clifton Road, where he stayed for many years. In May 1927, as soon as he was asked to join the War Memorial Gallery committee, he quickly became the key figure responsible for selecting and approving artwork for the gallery's permanent collection – a position he went on to hold for twelve years. In a letter by a fellow Education Committee member, Mr WA Robinson, he was once described as "Mr Chettle, the art expert of the committee".

The Gallery's Permanent Collection

On 21st November 1927, Chettle wrote a report to his colleagues on the Committee about a painting that had been offered to the gallery's permanent collection by Mr W Blundell of Great Portwood Street, Stockport:

"I have carefully inspected this oil painting by J Jones Barker dated 1881; it has a certain amount of merit, and no doubt as a family portrait would have some value, but as a work of art to be hung in the permanent collection, it has not sufficient merit, either of design or execution, to be desirable, and I regret I cannot advise its acceptance."

In the same report he also wrote a review of a white marble sculpture dated 1863 and entitled 'Play: Miss Hartree and Dog' by the renowned London artist Henry Weekes RA. It had been donated by a Mrs E Rayner who is noted as being the wife of Dr Rayner of Tiviot Dale. The sculpture is of a girl playing ball with her dog. She is holding a ball in her right hand and there is a quiver of arrows at her feet. It is believed that the theme of the sculpture is based on Diana the Huntress. Chettle's review reads:

"The sculpture is well-designed and carried out with considerable technical skill; like all the works of that period it is overloaded with detail and loses in this way some of the effect it is intended to convey. As a work of art it is much better than most of the examples to be seen of this period, in fact, I should describe it as a good example of a bad period. After carefully thinking the matter over I suggest that the committee accept this gift to be placed in the recess facing the stairs leading to the upper gallery, or on the landing near the entrance to the upper gallery."

The sculpture is still owned by Stockport Council, but is not currently on display.

Chettle was clearly a formidable character with a lot of business acumen and determined to make his mark. He had very definite views on what the relationship should be between the municipal authority and art, saying:

"The one thing that is necessary to develop the usefulness of our art gallery is the voting of a sum of money each year to enable the committee to add to the permanent collection. At the present time the gallery is entirely dependent on gifts, some of which are very undesirable, and loan collections. What we should do is to add to the permanent collection, and to do that adequately it is necessary to have some kind of annual grant – a small one of £200 would go a long way to begin with."

Fig 21: 'Play: Miss Hartree and Dog' by Henry Weekes RA (1863) – currently in storage in Stockport.

The Education Committee set out the following key principles for the use of the War Memorial building:

- To encourage the love of the beautiful as typified by the periodical Arts and Crafts
- To hold exhibitions in the minor galleries downstairs and to house the permanent art collection in the large gallery upstairs
- To deliver lectures and other educational meetings
- To perpetuate the names of the fallen Stockport men who made the supreme sacrifice.

Shortly after the building was opened, The Manchester Guardian wrote favourably about it, saying:

> *"this wholly charming little gallery is certainly worth more than a passing visit. Recently built, it has a freshness which is lacking in so many other local 'institutions', and it welcomes you straight from the hideous externals of Stockport without any flunkeyed officiousness into its cool, well-proportioned, friendly entrance halls, while upstairs it keeps a more dignified and stately gallery for sterner stuff."*

In the autumn of 1927 the War Memorial Gallery Committee, led by Chettle, sent out an invitation for artists to submit work for a forthcoming exhibition of 'Modern British Art' that would open straight after the Guild's exhibition had finished. Artists that were accepted for this prestigious show included Mary McNicoll Wroe (1861-1955), G Wood, GH James ARCA and, not too surprisingly, James Chettle. The exhibition opened on Monday 19th December 1927 and was unveiled by The Right Hon. Earl of Crawford and Balcarras. Chettle spoke at the opening ceremony about the work in the show, as well as their impressive permanent collection, and gave a vote of thanks to the Mayor and the Earl.

The Guild and the Gallery

The SGAC continued to hold its Annual Exhibition in the town's Masonic Meeting Hall until the beginning of 1927. Harry Garner and Tom Scott had settled into sharing the Chairmanship of the Stockport Guild. Other members of the council included:

Vice-Chairman Alfred Blackman; Honorary Treasurer John Sandiford and Honorary Secretary Miss Anne Nuttall.

In a letter dated 21st July 1927, Arthur Lawton, the Secretary of Education in Stockport, wrote to Anne Nuttall giving formal approval to "hold the Annual Exhibition of the Stockport Guild of Arts & Crafts in the Lower Gallery of the War Memorial Buildings during the month of November 1927." This was a landmark moment in Stockport Guild's history; they had been given the honour to grace the walls of the new War Memorial Art Gallery – an arrangement that would continue uninterrupted between the Gallery and the Guild for the next eighty years.

The Art Guild's 8th Annual Exhibition was split between the two downstairs rooms, with oil paintings in the east gallery and watercolours in the west. The exhibition included some figurative studies and landscape paintings by a 24-year-old artist from Hyde called Harry Rutherford (1903-1985), one of which was a striking portrait in tempera of a young boy in a cricket shirt and shorts. Also in the show was artwork by James Chettle and craftwork by Hugh Wallis.

The Manchester Guardian wrote about the exhibition, saying that:

> "Eight years ago a small group of enthusiasts founded the Stockport Guild of Arts & Crafts, and an interesting exhibition representing the work of nearly sixty members which was opened yesterday afternoon by the Mayor of Stockport is evidence of the steady development of the movement.
>
> The aims of the Guild are twofold, to stimulate and develop local interest in pictorial and decorative art and to place those who practice it in touch with the general public. Crowds of visitors on the first day suggest that these aims are being fulfilled.
>
> The new Memorial Gallery, with its two well-lit and pleasantly spaced rooms divided by a pillared hall, forms an ideal setting for such an exhibition, and by strictly limiting the number of pictures hung, the Selection Committee have raised the standard of the exhibits to a good level and prevented overcrowding."

The Stockport Advertiser also reviewed the show saying that the:

"Stockport Guild of Arts & Crafts Annual Exhibition is notable for a continuance of the high standard of work done by this local society in recent years. In the crafts section there are some very beautiful exhibits, and in the art section, whilst there are few works of transcending merit, the general level of quality is remarkably high, and maintains the progress that has been the outstanding feature of each exhibition.

Dealing with the less ambitious work first, local interest attached to a series of sketches by T Scott, of Manchester, notably 'The Old Fishing Tackle Shop.' The artist also has a painting of Manchester Cathedral. Number 109 by H Garner is worthy of special mention. It shows the remarkably picturesque scene of Stockport Market with the Parish Church in the background, the market hall to the left and the brightly coloured wares of the fruit stalls in the foreground. A scene of great beauty, which occurring under our eyes week after week usually passes unnoticed."

Some of the key players running both the Guild and the Gallery spoke at the opening of the exhibition, including Guild President Harry Garner. In his parting sentence, Garner said that nothing would please the committee better than to have a continuous series of such exhibitions in the building. Right there and then, the society had declared their ambitions in front of all the town's movers and shakers.

Chettle remained as the most influential person at the Education Committee for many years, inspecting every work of art and exhibition proposal that was presented to them. The Stockport Guild realised very quickly that, if they wanted to be a regular feature on the walls of the gallery, they needed to remain on good terms with Mr Chettle.

On the 26th January 1929, Garner chaired Stockport Guild's annual AGM at the Masonic Hall on Greek Street. During the meeting, Joseph Knowles proposed that members should be able to submit an unlimited number of works into the Guild's Annual Exhibition. Harry Rutherford disagreed, proposing that only four works should be allowed in. After much debate, it was agreed unanimously that the number of works 'may not exceed six and any or all of which may be hung.'

From the outset, the Stockport Guild believed in having both a pictorial section and a craft section in their Annual Exhibition. This was in keeping with the founding principles of the Arts & Crafts Exhibition Society, set out by Walter Crane, to promote decorative arts alongside fine arts. Crane's goal was for the public to ignore the

Fig 22: 'Wellington Road South, Stockport' by Harry Garner (circa 1913).

artificial distinction between Fine and Decorative Art:

"...the real distinction was what we conceived to be between good and bad art, or false and true taste and methods in handicraft, considering it of little value to endeavour to classify art according to its commercial value or social importance, while everything depended upon the spirit as well as the skill and fidelity with which the conception was expressed, in whatever material, seeing that a worker earned the title of artist by the sympathy with and treatment of his material, by due recognition of its capacity, and its natural limitations, as well as of the relation of the work to use and life."

It was no surprise then, that it was also agreed at Stockport Guild's 1929 AGM that a covering letter should be sent out to their members listing all the exhibition regulations, and in particular highlighting that the Annual Show 'is firstly an exhibition and secondly a sale.'

Crane's ethos clearly remained strong in Garner's mind.

The Stockport Guild of Arts & Crafts held its 10th Annual Exhibition in the War Memorial Gallery in November 1929. A number of prominent local artists were asked to be part of the pictorial section judging panel that year including Manchester artists Mary McNicoll Wroe, Lancelot Roberts RCA and an up and coming artist by the name of LS Lowry (1887 – 1976). It is reported that they were each paid 10/6 towards their expenses.

The exhibition had almost 10,000 visitors during its run and was deemed by Stockport Guild to be a huge success. Their secretary commented on it in her address at their AGM the following month:

"This year's exhibition was quite up to the standard as regards quality of work, but the full support of members had been extended as regards entries. Always did an Exhibition raise many controversial points – it was only at this General Meeting that these problems and difficulties be dealt with in both the Pictorial and Craft Sections of the Guild. Speaking of the Guild Class, held

in conjunction with the Stockport College, these and the summer sketching excursions had been quite successful."

Throughout the 1920s, the Stockport Guild organized a series of 'plein air' sketching and painting trips every summer to different places around the North West. The day out always concluded with a critique of everyone's work by one of the other members.

In 1929 the outings started in Stockport on the 4th May, with a critique by Harry Rutherford, who, by this time, was gaining quite a name for himself.

Harry Rutherford

Rutherford (1903-1985) was a keen artist from a young age and by his early teens had joined a Saturday morning class at Hyde School of Art led by a Stockport Guild member called Walter Potts.

Fig 23: The Portrait Class at the Manchester School of Art (circa 1923).

It is unclear whether Potts ignited Rutherford's interest in Arts and Crafts, but while he was still a teenager, Rutherford enrolled onto the 3-year Furniture and Interior Design evening course at the Manchester School of Art (MSoA). The head of the Fine Art department at MSoA at that time was Adolphe Valette, and, only a few years earlier, Walter Crane, founder of the Arts and Crafts Exhibition Society, had been Director of Design there.

Whilst Rutherford was at the School of Art, he won third prize in a national decorative design competition. So, with a growing interest both fine and applied arts, it's no surprise that, around this time, he joined the Stockport Guild of Arts & Crafts.

In 1923, Rutherford transferred to the Drawing and Painting Life course at the Manchester School of Art, which he subsequently attended four nights a week for a year. LS Lowry was a fellow student on the same course at this time. Rutherford recalls that Lowry, who had failed the course previously, wasn't taken very seriously back then.

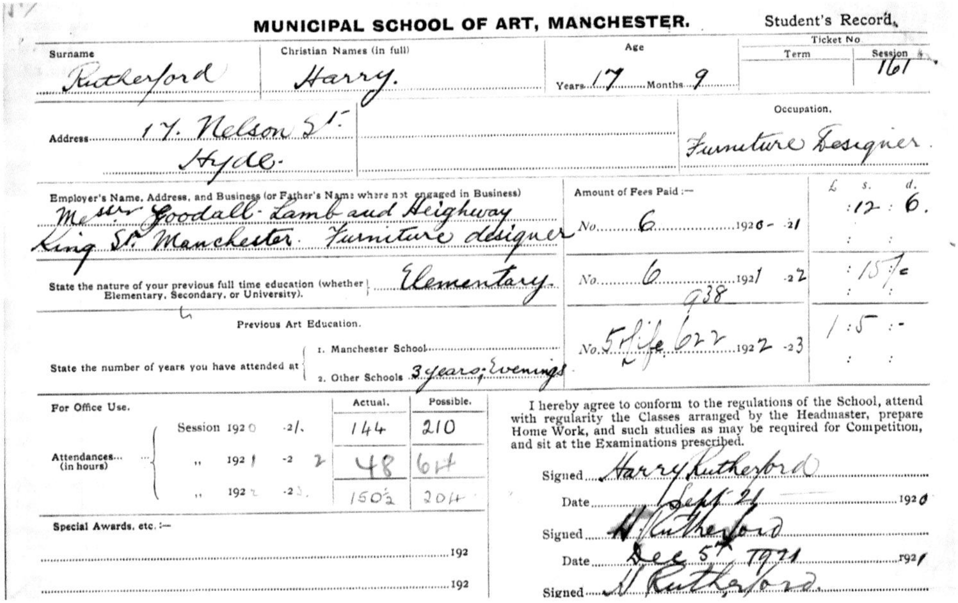
MUNICIPAL SCHOOL OF ART, MANCHESTER. Student's Record.

Surname: Rutherford
Christian Names (in full): Harry.
Age: Years 17 Months 9
Ticket No: Term / Session 161

Address: 17. Nelson St. Hyde.
Occupation: Furniture Designer.

Employer's Name, Address, and Business (or Father's Name where not engaged in Business): Messrs Goodall Lamb and Heighway King St. Manchester. Furniture designer

State the nature of your previous full time education (whether Elementary, Secondary, or University): Elementary.

Previous Art Education.
State the number of years you have attended at 1. Manchester School / 2. Other Schools: 3 years; Evenings

Amount of Fees Paid:
No. 6 1920-21 £ s. d. 12 : 6.
No. 6 1921-22 15/-
No. 5 Life 622 1922-23 1 : 5 : -

For Office Use.

Attendances (in hours)	Actual.	Possible.
Session 1920-21.	144	210
" 1921-22	48	64
" 1922-23	150½	204

Special Awards, etc.:—
192
192

I hereby agree to conform to the regulations of the School, attend with regularity the Classes arranged by the Headmaster, prepare Home Work, and such studies as may be required for Competition, and sit at the Examinations prescribed.

Signed Harry Rutherford
Date Sept 21 1920
Signed H Rutherford
Date Dec 5th 1921 1921
Signed H Rutherford

Fig 24: Rutherford's student records at the Manchester School of Art 1920-23.

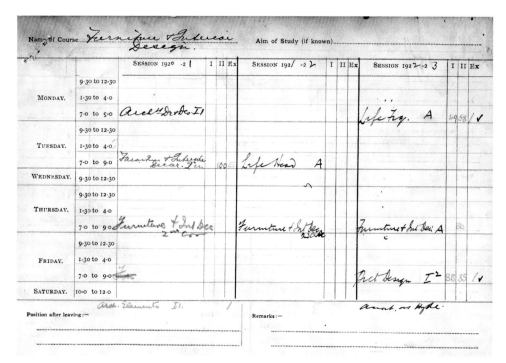

Fig 25: Rutherford's student records at the Manchester School of Art 1923-24.

(In January 1925, Rutherford switched to a private art school in St Mary's Parsonage, Manchester, which had just been set up by the renowned London painter Walter Sickert. He was the first and youngest of thirty pupils to sign up for his weekly life drawing and painting class. Other students that enrolled at the same time included James Chettle, William Reekie and Margaret Pilkington.

Sickert insisted that his class did small life sketches in tiny sketchbooks, which was unpopular with many of the students who had turned up with large canvases. Sickert also hired down-and-outs as life models instead of professionals and would also often pose as the model himself at the end of each lesson. The methods that Rutherford learned from Sickert suited him, especially his life sketches.

Interestingly, there was never any nude life drawing and painting, as Sickert's view was that people wear clothes and more practice in rapid drawing can be obtained from clothed figures because the folds of textiles are never the same twice. In Rutherford's 1925 painting "The Model, Sickert's Class", you can see the tones are muted and that the paint has been applied thinly. Rutherford liked the loose handling of paint and often left parts of his canvas untouched, part-defined and part-suggestive, something he was clearly taught to do by Sickert who also painted using this method.

By this stage Rutherford had become very close to his mentor, Sickert, to the extent that, at the end of 1925, when other work commitments drew Sickert back to London permanently, he selected Rutherford to take over the teaching of his class. Subsequently this was going to be run by the Manchester art dealer Charles Jackson and known as the 'Sickert Atelier.'

At the same time that Rutherford attended his evening classes, he also worked full-time in a series of other jobs. He was a lithographic printer, a furniture designer and later an artist for an advertising agency – this was as well as attending meetings and drawing sessions with the Stockport Guild of Arts & Crafts. He also freelanced as a 'topical cartoonist' for the Manchester Evening News, where he used his well-known sense of humour to capture the political satire of the day.

By January 1929, Rutherford was playing an increasingly active role in Stockport Guild and was elected onto their Executive Council.

Fig 26: 'The Model, Sickert's Class' by Harry Rutherford (1925).

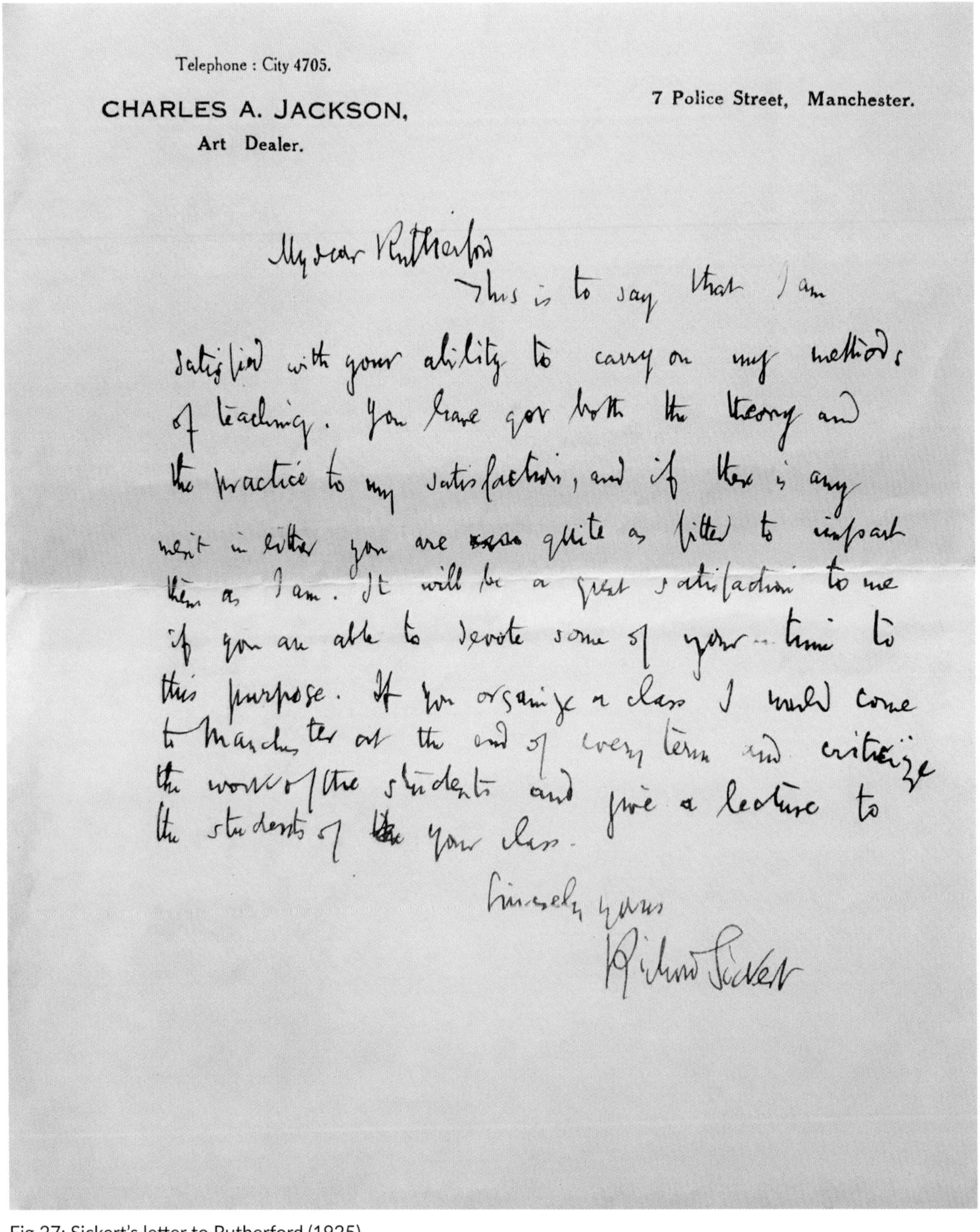

Telephone : City 4705.

CHARLES A. JACKSON,
Art Dealer.

7 Police Street, Manchester.

My dear Rutherford

This is to say that I am satisfied with your ability to carry on my methods of teaching. You have got both the theory and the practice to my satisfaction, and if there is any merit in either you are ~~xxxx~~ quite as likely to impart them as I am. It will be a great satisfaction to me if you are able to devote some of your time to this purpose. If you organize a class I would come to Manchester at the end of every term and criticize the work of the students and give a lecture to the students of ~~the~~ your class.

Sincerely yours
Richard Sickert

Fig 27: Sickert's letter to Rutherford (1925).

Fig 28: Harry Rutherford painting a portrait of Mr Samuel Ashworth (1929).

The
1930s

The Guild goes from Strength to Strength

Fig 29: 'Lyme Cage' by Clarence Northing (1930).

Harry Rutherford exhibited two paintings in the Stockport Guild of Arts & Crafts' Annual Exhibition in 1930 and continued to be a regular at Guild Council meetings that year. However, in 1931, Rutherford moved to London to work full-time as an illustrator and a cartoonist for a number of Fleet Street magazines.

Rutherford and Sickert had kept in regular contact and so it's possible that it was Sickert that persuaded Rutherfold to move down to London. Rutherford fleetingly visited Stockport at least twice in 1931, firstly to judge the pictorial section of the Guild's Annual Exhibition and then to attend the opening of the exhibition on the 24th October 1931. His impromptu 'retirement' from the Guild Council was formally ratified at the Society's AGM in 1932 and he was made an Honorary Member of the SGAC. He continued to exhibit in the Guild's Annual Exhibitions for a few more years.

In the Stockport Guild Exhibition of 1936, the catalogue listed his London address as Studio Four, 142 Brecknock Road, N7. There were six artist spaces in Brecknock Studios at that time. Although it's unknown who the other artists were in the building, one of them might well have been Walter Sickert, who had acquired a large top-lit studio in that street in Tufnell Park a few decades earlier.

The same year, Rutherford produced a commercial illustration for the front cover of The Listener Magazine, which resulted in him securing a job on a new light entertainment BBC TV show called 'Cabaret

Fig 30: 'September, Mottram' by Harry Rutherford (circa 1937)

Cartoons.' Rutherford was a regular feature on the show, drawing cartoon sketches of all the variety acts that were on the bill. The producer, Cecil Madden, however, never let Rutherford have a spoken part because, allegedly, his northern accent was inappropriate for the BBC!

By the early fifties Rutherford starred in his own children's television series, 'Sketchbook', which continued for six years. Towards the end of the run, Rutherford, who was 53 years old by then, had become disillusioned with his TV work in London and so decided to return to Hyde.

By 1957 he was teaching at the Manchester Regional College of Art. Rutherford had joined the Manchester Academy of Fine Arts in 1933, but in 1961 was unanimously elected as its President, a post he held for eight years.

Fig 31: Harry Rutherford in his room.

Fig 32: Harry Rutherford at his easel.

The Tom Scott Years

This was a time of significant change for the Stockport Guild. Under the leadership of Tom Scott (Chairman from 1930-46) membership numbers grew rapidly and the society desperately needed to become more structured in the way it was run.

In 1930, the Stockport Advertiser hailed the Society's 11th Annual Exhibition as a huge success, estimating that over 4,000 people visited their exhibition at the War Memorial Gallery on the opening Sunday alone.

> *"This is the Eleventh Annual Exhibition of its kind, and its object, as stated in the foreword to the catalogue 'is to bring together the people of Stockport and the artists and craftsmen living in their midst'."*

The paper went on to describe some of their favourite pieces in the exhibition:

> *"Walter Kirkman's 'Springtime' is a pleasant representation of a river running through a wood, and in JP Chettle's picture, 'Dawn,' various tints of grey predominate in a most effective manner. Davenport Bates's portrait of Mrs Bates is a really capital likeness, and the painting is in the artist's most felicitous manner. The most notable picture in the exhibition is H Rutherford's 'An English Country Market.' It depicts a sale of sheep, and the auctioneer and his assistants, as well as the numerous customers, are evidently careful presentations of different types, the counterparts of which can be seen at any country sale. Mr Rutherford also shows 'Summer in Romiley,' painted from the inside of a house window, evidently close to the Stock Dove Hotel."*

Interestingly, The Manchester Guardian gave a less complimentary review of some of the work at the show (or at least of the artists' view of their hometown):

> *"The Stockport painters do not despise their own city, which they paint with affection but without illusions. Mr William Shone's two small pictures are most successful in conveying the air of being grubby, but like home – Mr Lowry's pitiless industrialism is eschewed."*

William Shone

William Shone, a watercolourist from Yorkshire, was a key member of the Guild throughout the 1920s and 30s. He taught at the Bradford College of Art, just a few miles away from Shipley where Walter Foster was teaching. Shone was a Stockport Guild council member, exhibitor and sketching trip leader throughout the thirties. The meeting minute books from the time recorded that he led a number of summer outdoor sketching trips. On the 5th July 1930, he was in charge of a group trip to Disley for a day's plein air sketching. Later in life, Shone became a Fellow of the Royal Society of Arts, an award only granted to individuals that have outstanding achievements relating to the Arts.

Fig 33: 'Low Tide St. Ives' by William Shone FRSA.

Alderman Patten was Chairman of the War Memorial Gallery Committee by 1930 and he presided over the SAG's exhibition opening, where he said:

> "Most Corporations found it necessary to co-opt gentlemen on certain committees on account of their special knowledge. Just as Mr Reekie's advice was sought on the Manchester Art Gallery Committee, we in Stockport had co-opted Mr Chettle onto the War Memorial Committee, and were getting very valuable advice and help from him in connection with the exhibitions held in this building."

James Chettle, who was also at the event, said:

> "Exhibitions such as this were the centre round which all art societies revolved. They afforded opportunities for one painter to become acquainted with the work of others. In this Art Gallery during the last two years we have endeavoured to have a succession of interesting exhibitions of works, the study of which could not fail to be useful to any painter."

Another of Tom Scott's ideas was to introduce a monthly 'Drawing Circle', which ran in conjunction with their summer outdoor sketching programme. These were essentially life drawing sessions that took place either in Mr James' studio at the Stockport School of Art on Wellington Road or at Ronald Allan's studio in Heaton Moor.

Fig 34: Ronald Allan, Guild Council member during the 1930s.

Fig 35: Life session sketch by Ronald Allan.

Clarence Northing

One of the regular artists on the summer sketching programme was Clarence Northing who had been a member of the Stockport Guild since the early days. Born near Bradford in 1895, Northing left school at fourteen to work for a Fine Art Dealer where he learned to cut mounts and frame pictures. He studied art three times a week at night school.

Fig 36: Clarence Northing sketching en plein air in Wadsley (circa 1929).

He served on the front line during the First World War and was wounded in action and pensioned off for 18 months. He spent this time doing watercolour sketches in and around Bradford before moving to Romiley to start work in Manchester for the Boots art department. This was when he joined the Stockport Guild of Arts & Crafts.

Northing became one of the Society's most active and vocal members during the thirties, always happy to hold criticisms and lead sketching trips. He continued to play a key part in the Stockport Guild until his resignation on the 23rd October 1936. The Guild Council were disappointed to see him go and wrote a 'special letter of regret' to him expressing the committee's appreciation of services rendered and saying that they hoped he would renew his membership in the future.

Within a few months, Northing founded a breakaway art society, called the Romiley Art Group, and brought with him a several other artists from the Stockport Guild of Arts & Crafts.

Fig 29: Northing Lyme Cage (circa 1930).

Arts versus Crafts

In 1932, Lawrence Haward, curator of the Manchester Art Gallery, opened the Guild's 13th Annual Exhibition at the War Memorial Gallery. Controversially, the craft section was only given one week to display their work, whereas a whole month had been allocated to the pictorial section. For the first time in the history of the Stockport Guild of Arts & Crafts a power struggle had begun to appear between the disciplines of decorative art and craftwork.

The Stockport Express described the show saying:

"On the whole the exhibition is well up on the standard of former years, and in figure painting there is undoubtedly a distinct advantage on previous achievements.

Mr GH James ARCA, Principle of the Arts and Crafts School at Stockport College, has five examples on view, four portraits and an 'Interior with Objects.' Ronald Allen's representation of 'The Oldest Inhabitant' will undoubtedly cause much comment and some criticism. It is a somewhat weird picture. The old man has white hair and beard and a very ruddy countenance, and his body is clothed in a blue suit. The rest of the picture consists of areas of vivid pink, yellow and green, without any detail."

The Manchester Guardian observed that:

"Membership of the Guild is not confined exclusively to Stockport, and there are exhibitors from Wilmslow, Whalley Range, Hyde, Prestbury, Buxton and even wider afield. The honours in the oil section are shared by GH James, principal of the Stockport School of Art, who is represented by four portraits and a still-life study; and James P Chettle, a Manchester businessman, who shows four landscapes. 'The Green Blouse' is the best of Mr James's work, while Mr Chettle is best represented by 'One Fine Day' and 'Grey Day, Boston'."

Other exhibitors that year included: Frederick Davenport Bates, Wallace Ardern, Elsie Ward, Harry Garner, William Shone, Walter Potts, Frank Escourt, Walter Kirkman,

Hugh Wallis, Tom Scott and Ernest Pickford.

Ernest Pickford

One of the exhibitors in the Guild's 13th Annual Exhibition in 1932 was Ernest Pickford.

Pickford trained in Architectural Design at the Manchester School of Art. After qualifying, he moved to Stockport and began working remotely for the eminent Arts and Crafts metalworking company, the Bromsgrove Guild of Applied Arts (who famously made Liverpool's Liver birds and the gates at Buckingham Palace). He also worked on the design for the Stourbridge war memorial with the Manchester-based sculptor John Cassidy. Pickford exhibited with the Stockport Guild for the last time in 1932. At the Council meeting on the 9th December, the honorary treasurer, John Sandiford, informed the members present of Pickford's resignation from the membership.

Tom Scott's modernisation of the Stockport Guild continued unabated into 1933. Ahead of that year's exhibition Scott promoted James Chettle to Vice-President of the Society - interestingly coinciding with the first time that the Guild had been granted use of the whole of the War Memorial Gallery.

The 1933 exhibition had seventy-four oil paintings on show, including what was to become one of Harry Rutherford's most iconic pictures entitled 'London Night, 1933.' In Chettle's address at the exhibition opening he compared it with the best pictures that had been shown in the gallery and said that he:

"Strongly advised the 'city fathers' to purchase it for the permanent collection. For the benefit of those who are economically inclined, the price of the picture is so modest that it would have but an infinitesimal effect on the rates, and also it might prove a good investment from a financial point of view, for as the artist's fame grows the value of his pictures will naturally increase and what may be purchased today for what is really a mere song may in a few years be worth considerably more."

The Manchester Guardian highlighted another Rutherford painting in the show saying:

> "The picture which seems most arresting upon first inspection is Harry Rutherford's painting of Buxton. We are given a view of the crescent beyond a foreground of circular paths in whose green enclosures thin bare trees are seen looking a little unhappy in Buxton's winter sunshine. Beyond the green roofs of the Crescent and the hospital curvilinear roads rise to the hills. The buildings are precise, cold, still, and formal; they are seen with great detachment, with understanding and a lovely appreciation of shapes and it seems the painter has epitomized Buxton. The town ought to possess this picture."

Margaret Pilkington, the founder of the Red Rose Guild, was also a member of the Stockport Guild at this time. She exhibited an etching from Sicily in the 1933 show that was said to have 'an almost fairytale brevity and exactitude of balance

Fig 37: Wood Engraving by Margaret Pilkington (1924).

Fig 38: Wood Engraving by Margaret Pilkington (1924).

in it.' Frederick Davenport Bates exhibited a portrait in the exhibition that year of Councillor Frank Brown, JP, a very familiar Stockport figure at the time.

Fig 39: Councillor Frank Brown, JP, by Frederick Davenport Bates (1933).

Mr and Mrs Scott's home at 1 Crosby Street (just around the corner from the War Memorial Gallery) had been a regular venue for Stockport Guild's monthly council meetings but at the gathering in September 1934, Scott announced that the house had been sold and that that was going to be their last council meeting there. At the session, everyone was informed that Stockport's Mayor, who was due to unveil the Annual Exhibition in a few weeks' time, was now indisposed indefinitely and so Chettle was asked if he would be happy to open the show instead.

One month later at the opening of the 15th Annual Exhibition in 1934, Chettle delivered a speech that dwelt on the value of the Stockport Guild of Arts and Crafts and ended with an impassioned appeal that "every artist, craftsmen and painter should belong to a society like this." Chettle had four paintings on display that year including a picture of boats in a harbour entitled 'Sharpness.' Rutherford also sent a couple of paintings up from London, one called 'A Window in Northern Spain' and another called 'My Brother Playing.' William Shone submitted 'The Dole' and Mr CW Van Der Veen showed 'Willow Pattern.'

The Manchester Guardian reported that:

> "Artists from a wide area have contributed works, and at least four of the pictures have come from a Stockport artist now working in London, Mr H Rutherford. One of them, "The Harbour, La Coruna," ranks with Mr Chettle's 'sharpness' as the best of the oils. Mr Davenport Bates's portrait, "John Fletcher," remains true to tradition, while Mr GH James is best represented by the portrait, No. 6, although one has seen stronger work from his brush."

Once again the crafters were only given a week to show their work, whereas the fine artists had been given a month. It's not surprising then that the show consisted of 217 exhibits: 203 were pictures and only 14 pieces made up the craft section. The battle for fine art's supremacy over craftwork was about to be decided.

Fig 40: (l to r) Tom Scott, Mr Stanley, Mr Estcourt, Miss Kirk and Mary McNicholl Wroe study a painting by Harry Rutherford in the 1938 annual Stockport Art Guild exhibition.

Dropping the Craft

On Saturday 3rd February 1934, fine artist Clarence Northing stood up at the AGM and declared that for a number of years the Society had generally been referred to as 'The Stockport Guild,' and proposed that it was time the name of the 'Stockport Guild of Arts & Crafts' was formally abbreviated to 'The Stockport Guild.' Following a debate with fellow members, including Walter Kirkman, William Shone, Tom Scott, Annie Storey and Edith Hamlett, the idea of shortening the society's name was formally rejected.

At the AGM the following year Clarence Northing resubmitted his proposal, this time asking for their name to be altered to "Stockport Art Guild." Despite fierce objection from craftworkers' Annie Storey and Edith Hamlett, the vote went almost unanimously in favour of the name change and on the 9th February 1935, Stockport Art Guild (SAG) was born.

At the SAG Council meeting in October that year, Anne Nuttall stood up and proposed a motion "that the Executive Council have the power to invite up to six artists from contemporary societies to exhibit pictorial work, should our own Guild members be unable to produce necessary work." It was carried unanimously. Nuttall said she would meet with James Chettle to arrange details of the exhibition selection and hanging. Tom Scott was clearly determined to make sure, at all costs, that the newly named Stockport 'Art' Guild put on a spectacular pictorial exhibition.

> 'Stockport Art Guild' was the succinct headline that ran in The Manchester Guardian on the 2nd December 1935. In the article the paper said that the Guild:
>
> "...has an interesting innovation this year in the inclusion of specimens of work by non-members of the Guild, with a view to arousing greater keenness on the part of members and those visiting the exhibition."

The Manchester Academy of Fine Arts (MAFA) had successfully trialled a similar amendment to their constitution a couple of years previously, whereby non-MAFA members could submit work for inclusion into their Annual Spring Exhibition. The effect was that it gave their organisation a fresh injection of vitality and encouraged a wider range of artists to apply for membership. Maybe this was something that Stockport Guild Vice-President and MAFA President Chettle had brought to the Art Guild's attention?

Fig 41: James Chettle at the opening of the Stockport Guild Annual Exhibition in 1934.

The foreword in the SAG annual exhibition catalogue that year attempted to justify the dropping of 'Crafts' in the name:

"In our opening exhibition three years ago, Mr Lawrence Hayward expressed his satisfaction at seeing so many branches of art brought together in one show and so helping to break down the invidious distinctions between 'fine' and 'applied' art. We have always tried to keep this ideal in the forefront of our minds and to give as broad and comprehensive a range as possible to our exhibition."

Behind closed doors, the Guild Council appeared to have a different view. After the show they discussed the merits (or lack) of some of the craftworkers and regretted allowing one particular craft member to exhibit 'some brass and copper work'. They also decided that another craftworker and a lacemaker would only be allowed to exhibit in future as individuals but not as SAG members. Clearly the presence of craft members continued to present an unreasonable conundrum for the Guild leadership.

Frederick Davenport Bates

One of the more notable artists that exhibited in the Stockport Guild's 1935 exhibition was the well-known local painter Frederick 'Davenport' Bates. His painting of 'Marple Locks' gained extra recognition when it was published in the Stockport Advertiser. The newspaper caption reads: A critical scrutiny of Mr F Davenport Bates' picture of Marple Locks at the Stockport Art Guild's Exhibition in the War Memorial Art Gallery.

Fig 42: 'Marple Locks' by Frederick Davenport Bates (1935) .

Fig 43: (l to r) Mr RA Dawson (Principle of the Manchester School of Art), James Chettle, Tom Scott, Mr JT Stanley, Councillor Miss CE Johnson and Councillor W Noble with Frederick 'Davenport' Bates painting of Marple Locks (1935).

Frederick 'Davenport' Bates was born in 1867 in Chorlton-on-Medlock. By the age of twenty-one he had decided to pursue a career as an artist and moved to Paris to study in the ateliers of Boulevard St.Michel. In 1888, he became a student at the hugely popular Académie Julian, and here, alongside aspiring artists from all around the world, he was taught classically by tutors Adolphe William Bouguereau (1825–1905), Tony Robert-Fleury and Gabriel Ferrier.

Frederick Davenport Bates was christened Frederick Bates. He added the middle name 'Davenport' when he moved to the Stockport suburb at the beginning of the twentieth century, not only as a badge of pride for the area, but also to distinguish him from another artist of the same name.

Writing about Académie Julian, John Russell, the celebrated New York Times Art critic wrote:

"By my count, more than 50 nationalities were represented at the school during its glory years. To be at the Académie Julian was to be exposed to a kind of white magic that seems to have worked in almost every case. What was learned there stayed forever with alumnus and alumna, and it related as much to the conduct of life as to the uses of brush and chisel."

It was at Académie Julian that Davenport Bates learnt his craft by drawing and painting from life models everyday from dawn til dusk. During the time he studied there, the term 'L'art pompier' had started to be used in Paris as a

Fig 44: Académie Julian circa 1891.

derisive term for the traditional academic teaching methods that Académie Julian used. As a result, the art school adopted a more liberal and less conservative 'Florentine' approach.

As well as his extremely accomplished portraits and religious paintings, Davenport Bates became known for turning his hand to popular local landscapes, such as the study of Marple Locks that he exhibited in SAG's Exhibition of 1935.

After spending time in Antwerp and North Africa, by the beginning of the twentieth century Davenport Bates had returned to the Britain and was living in Davenport with Catherine, his new wife. He became a passionate supporter of both Davenport and Stockport. He was one of the founders of the Stockport Literary Club, took a keen interest in the work of the Stockport Lads' Club and was an early and valued member of the Stockport Art Guild.

Davenport Bates died at his home in Mile End Lane, Stockport, on the 17th July 1943. A couple of months later, at the Art Guild Council meeting on 3rd September, it was agreed that, Catherine, Frederick's widow, would be approached by Tom Scott to see if she would be willing to allow the Art Guild to display a memorial exhibition of his work.

Fig 45: 'Alderman William Lees' by Frederick Davenport Bates.

A Spectacular Exhibition

By 1936 Stockport Art Guild was being run by an impressive panel of Vice-Presidents including James Chettle and Alderman Charles Royle - who were also both running the Memorial Gallery at that time.

The Guild's exhibition catalogue that year had an introduction from Tom Scott that read:

> *"We would venture to suggest that there is no Annual Exhibition in this district at which there are so many branches of artwork, and so much variety within those branches, as a Guild exhibition."*

Fig 46: 17th Annual Exhibition catalogue (1936).

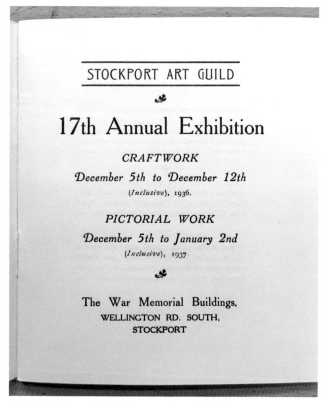

Fig 47: 17th Annual Exhibition catalogue (1936).

There were 234 works in the show and the catalogue cited that the work had come from artists as far and wide as London, Lancashire, Merseyside and Manchester. Professor Webster of Manchester University opened the Annual Exhibition in 1936, observing that:

> *"The Guild makes steady progress. While the skill of members with pencil and paint is shown with definite steps each year, the craft section's progress is even more rapid. Silver, metal, woodwork and weaving provide strong competition."*

The craftsmen might have fallen out of favour with certain members of SAG, but they clearly still had some support, albeit from outside the Guild.

The Stockport Art Guild and the Manchester Academy of Fine Arts

Several prominent artists from the Manchester Academy of Fine Arts took part in the Guild's 1936 exhibition: James Chettle showed several Dorset-inspired paintings; Marjorie Mort had four pieces in the show; Mr CW Van Der Veen exhibited a number of studio oil paintings and a couple of plein air watercolours from recent travels; Harry Rutherford sent up two oils from London (including one of his seminal works called 'Durham Morning') and Mary McNicoll Wroe, who had also been accepted as a Full Member of the Stockport Art Guild the previous year, exhibited three watercolours.

Fig 48: Mary McNicoll Wroe.

Fig 49: 'Schoolgirl' by Mary McNicholl Wroe (circa 1901).

Fig 50: Watercolour of Manchester Cathedral interior by Mary McNicholl Wroe (1922).

The artist community in Manchester was close-knit, especially the MAFA members. Mary McNicoll Wroe, an accomplished watercolourist and good friend of James Chettle, painted a beautifully observed portrait of him during their time together at the MAFA.

Fig 51: 'Old Swanage, Dorset' by James Chettle (1936).

James Chettle waited until the start of the 1930s to join the Manchester Academy of Fine Arts. Up until 1917 MAFA was an association confined to 'Professional Painters, Sculptors, Architects and Engravers born or having resided for not less than twelve months within a radius of 20 miles from the Town Hall of Manchester.' The rule change that allowed amateurs into the Academy was a key turning point for Chettle. By 1930 he had been elected as a Full Member of MAFA and three years later he was elected as their Vice-President. The following year, in 1934, he achieved the incredible accolade of being the first amateur artist to become President. The Stockport Advertiser described his rise to fame as an artist as 'meteoric.'

After the 1936 exhibition, Tom Scott received a kind letter from Chettle congratulating the Stockport Art Guild on the standard of the show and commenting on the increasing attraction of the Guild's exhibitions.

The Guild on the Up

As Stockport Art Guild became more established, a feeling began to grow amongst the membership that more space was needed in the War Memorial Gallery to display their work. The following extract is taken from the minutes of Tom Scott's Chairman's address at their 1936 AGM:

"By the majority of townspeople, the Stockport Art Guild is welcomed as a sign of aesthetic culture. In the past there appeared to be some doubt with regard to the use of the Upper Gallery."

Scott went on to say that he looked forward to the time when it would be taken for granted that they would have full use of all the gallery space. Councillor Kate Johnson attended the 1936 exhibition and remarked that SAG's position should be asserted and the use of the Upper Gallery demanded. Stockport Art Guild was beginning to take hold of the cultural life within the town.

By the AGM the following year, the right to use the Upper Gallery was established and it now became clear that despite the Guild's grand plans, there might not be sufficient members to fill the space. In 1937, membership levels were only: 58 Pictorial, 11 Craft (with 9 classed as joint) and 3 honorary members.

Fig 52: A 14" x 10" watercolour of James Chettle by fellow MAFA member Mary McNicoll Wroe.

Wilfred Colclough

The Stockport Guild received an application for membership in July 1937 from a well-known local artist called Wilfred J. Colclough. He was duly accepted. Colclough was an accomplished amateur painter and had an eye for capturing the raw beauty of a rugged landscape in the British hills. In the Guild's 1942 exhibition he exhibited a series of local scenes entitled 'Pines, Alderley Edge' 'Langdale Pikes', 'Spring Fantasy' and 'Jitterbugs.'

By 1944, Colclough had reluctantly become the Guild's Honorary Secretary and had taken over the planning of their annual summer sketching programmes and managing the membership – a role he performed for ten years. He continued to be actively involved and to exhibit with SAG every year for over half a century (more than any other member). Aside from painting and his long involvement in the Guild, Colclough spent the majority of his career as a schoolteacher at Stockport School, later becoming the school's historian.

During the researching of this book a rather sad poem, signed by Wilfred Colclough, was discovered hidden amongst the Guild's old meeting minutes - it's called "Stockport 1938" (shown opposite).

The rule to invite non-members to exhibit in the Annual Exhibition was retracted in 1937 and SAG's 18th Annual Exhibition became a member-only show once more. However, one custom that did remain was the bias towards fine art - as usual, the craftworkers were only given one week to exhibit their work.

Walter Potts dominated the pictorial section of the 1937 show with several excellent watercolours of Derbyshire landscapes. Chettle also had a couple on show, 'Derbyshire' and 'The Wind and the Rain.' At a meeting a few months later, the Guild Council expressed "great satisfaction on hearing of the sale of pictures by Mr Rutherford and Mr Potts at the last exhibition."

Stockport 1938

This town,
One up, two down
Many steps, a square,
Wet roofs, pavement bare,
Narrow alleys, dirty river,
Gaunt mills, street lights quiver,
Hotch-potch, ragged, no design,
Grimy chapel, thought sublime,
Noisy trains, "Inside only",
Unemployed, lifeless, lonely,
Evening paper – nothing new,
"Bar in Spain", "County drew",
Picture theatre, neon-lighted,
Film-struck patrons, tense excited,
Duped folk, narrow-minded,
To vital issues, indifferent, blinded.

Nothing planned – confusion.

Walter Potts

Walter Potts (1883 – 1965) was a well-respected art teacher, watercolourist and sculptor from Glossop. He was a stalwart of the Manchester art scene, both as a teacher and an artist, for most of his life. From the turn of the twentieth century he taught at the Hyde School of Art for over forty years. One of Potts' pupils there was Harry Rutherford; a talented youngster who would one day become Stockport Art Guild's most renowned artist.

Potts' professional teaching career really took off when he was appointed Art Master at Stockport Grammar School in 1915, just after the Old Grammar School had moved from its building on Greek Street to a brand new facility on Buxton Road (where the school is today). He also continued as head of Hyde School of Art and remained in both posts until his retirement in 1948.

As an artist, he is probably best known for his soft and delicately captured landscapes and rural compositions that often featured a quaint village or half-timbered house. He also painted miniatures and some of them are reported to have been exhibited in the Royal Academy.

He regularly attended the Art Guild from the 1930s and by the end of that decade was on the Guild's Executive Council, a role that he retained for over ten years.

Fig 53: 'Old Flemish House, Tenby' by Walter Potts (circa 1938).

Such was the importance of figures like Potts and Rutherford to the Art Guild during the thirties that the following comment was officially minuted at the Council meeting on April 9th 1938:

'The Council expressed great satisfaction on hearing of the sale of pictures by Mr Rutherford and Mr Potts at the last exhibition.' It's great to think that Harry Rutherford, the boy he taught from a young age, was exhibiting shoulder to shoulder on the walls of the Memorial Gallery thanks to the Art Guild.

We know that Potts and Rutherford had a warm and friendly relationship. When Ken Howarth, the founder of the Northwest Sound Archive, interviewed Harry Rutherford he described Walter Potts as an "extremely kind man and gifted watercolourist."

Potts was clearly very popular, not only at the Art Guild, and was always happy to lend his support to other groups and organisations. He often helped the Stockport Dramatic Society paint the scenery for their plays; regularly designed posters for local publicity campaigns and was repeatedly commissioned to create paintings for Stockport Council's outgoing chairmen. He was elected into the Manchester Academy of Fine Arts in 1935.

However, in March 1941, Potts tendered his resignation from the Art Guild Council. This was a shock to the other Council members and at the next meeting it was proposed and seconded that he should be invited to become a Vice-President of the Guild. He duly accepted and on Friday 18th July 1941 Walter Potts was sworn in. By this time he was exhibiting regularly and had added AMC, FRSA to his name.

In 1949, a year after his retirement from Stockport Grammar School, he was asked to design the school gates. The design he came up with incorporated the shield of the school's founder (one or the earliest coats of arms to be registered with the College of Heralds), the motto of the school and some beautiful floral work.

Fig 54: Stockport Grammar School gates, designed by Walter Potts.

Walter Potts exhibited with the Art Guild until 1959 and sadly passed away 6 years later in 1965, aged 82. Stockport Grammar School wrote an obituary that read:

"Walter Potts will chiefly live through his watercolours which were always sound and reflected the gentle and lovable character of their maker. There are many well-known painters now working who owe him a debt of gratitude for their early training and generations of Stockport Grammar School boys who will always remember with affection the personality of Walter Potts."

Today several of Potts' paintings are in private and public collections in and around Manchester, including some key works that still hang on the walls at Stockport Grammar School.

Fig 55: 'Rhythm' by Walter Potts in Stockport Guild's Annual Exhibition in 1938.

SAG Members see Red

In 1938, Stockport Guild's Annual Exhibition had earned the right to use the larger Upper Gallery of the War Memorial Building. To help fill the space, the Guild Council decided to invite The Red Rose Guild of Crafters to exhibit alongside them. Margaret Pilkington and Hugh Wallis, both still SAG members, had been very successful with their Red Rose Guild and it had become a well-regarded society with a higher national profile than Stockport Art Guild. Harold and Phoebe Stabler, leading craft exponents of the time, were amongst the celebrated crafters who exhibited.

Despite this, there were still a number of complaints from some of the SAG membership about unwanted 'outside crafters' being allowed to share the gallery. Their complaints, however, were not upheld since the craftwork section proved very popular with the public.

Fig 56: Judging of Stockport Guild's Annual Exhibition in 1938 at the War Memorial Gallery.

Frederick Davenport Bates and Harry Rutherford dominated the pictorial section of the show. Davenport Bates showed a portrait of Judge TB Leigh, the Mayor of Stockport (who also opened the exhibition), which was presented to him on completion of fifty years' service as a Stockport teacher. Rutherford exhibited a painting of a sporty-looking gentleman wearing a bowler hat called 'Harry Herbert.'

The Stockport Advertiser described it as a:

> "Belcher-like study with the richness and rubicundity
> of the Belcher colourings. But it is a first-rate piece of
> work. Unfortunately it is hung far above the eye-level
> of the normal beholder and is only by standing on a
> chair that one sees the subject as the artist saw him.
> The other work, his delightful painting of Ammon
> Wrigley, the Saddleworth poet, amongst his beloved
> fells wreathed in mist, is more than a portrait. And,
> of course, in both cases Mr Rutherford's technical skill
> is impeccable."

Tom Scott had eight works on display that year; Mary
McNicoll Wroe submitted a couple of pictures and Walter
Potts exhibited a series of paintings as well as a sculpture of
a panther entitled 'Rhythm.'

Stockport Guild's working relationship with The Red Rose
Guild continued the following year when their show, which
was due to open in Houldsworth Hall, was cancelled at the
last minute. Margaret Pilkington, Hugh Wallis and around
twenty other members of the Red Rose Guild displayed
work in Stockport Art Guild's twentieth Annual Exhibition.
Lack of floor space prevented furniture from being exhibited
and so they populated the craft section with 'popular-priced'
articles.

Fig 57: James Chettle at his easel in 1938.

Pressed as they were for wall exhibits, the Guild still rigidly adhered to the rules and a number of late submissions were rejected. Chairman Mr Tom Scott commented that:

"...he greatly regretted that three well-known members had been unable to submit work – namely Mr James Chettle, Miss Marjorie Mort and Mr Van der Veen. Mr Chettle hoped to be able to send us some work next year. Mr Van der Veen's own private exhibition had unfortunately coincided with the Guild exhibition."

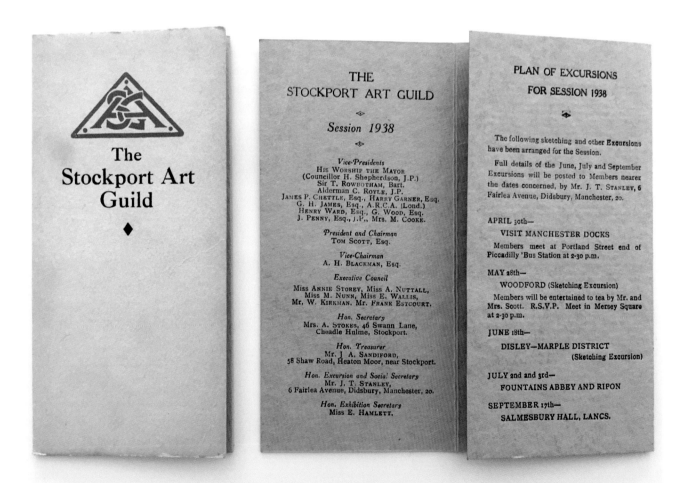

Fig 58: Stockport Art Guild Session Card from 1938.

Marjorie Mort

Marjorie Mort (1906 - 1989) studied art at the Manchester School of Art from 1924 to 1931. She was initially interested in decorative arts, but before long realised her true interest lay in fine art, especially drawing and painting the human figure. She then spent a few years living and working in London and Cornwall before moving up to Mellor in 1936 to teach at the Stockport School of Art seven miles away. She was elected as a member of Stockport Art Guild in 1939 and joined the Manchester Academy of Arts in 1941. After the end of the War, she moved back to Mousehole in Cornwall.

Fig 59: 'Factories' by Marjorie Mort (1935).

James Chettle took the decision to resign from the War Memorial Committee at the beginning of 1939. He cited that he had too many demands upon his time that he felt he could no longer sit upon the Gallery Committee, adding:

> *"I shall always be willing to do anything I can for them in an unofficial capacity. Stockport has one of the best War Memorials ever erected, and one of the nicest art galleries I have ever seen."*

The Stockport Advertiser commented that 'the town can ill afford to lose the services of such experts that live within its borders, and there can be no two opinions as to the high position which Mr Chettle holds in the art world.'

The same year, James and his wife Eleanor moved to a large 1930s-style house at 1 Ramsdale Road, Bramhall, where he lived until his death in December 1944.

Mr. J. P. Chettle

I WAS VERY SORRY to learn from the minutes of the Stockport Education Committee this week that Mr. J. P. Chettle, of Davenport Park, has severed his connection with the War Memorial Buildings sub-committee, for the town can ill-afford to lose the services of such experts as live within its borders, and there can be no two opinions as to the high position which Mr. Chettle holds in the art world.

He has been a member of the sub-committee which looks after the War Memorial Art Gallery since 1928, and his services as art adviser to the committee has been very valuable.

He tells me, however, that he has so many calls upon his time these days that he felt he could no longer sit upon the committee.

"I shall always be willing to do anything I can for them in an unofficial capacity," he said. "Stockport has one of the best war memorials ever erected, and one of the nicest art galleries I have ever seen."

His Hobby

ART is, of course, a hobby with Mr. Chettle, not a full-time occupation. "Nature intended me to be a painter, but necessity decreed that I should enter the cotton trade," he told me on a previous occasion.

He was elected President of the Manchester Academy of Fine Arts in 1934—the first amateur to be offered the position—and he still holds it.

The Academy's spring exhibition opened at the City Art Gallery on Monday this week, and Mr. Chettle is showing five paintings.

Fig 60: Chettle's departure in 1939 from the Stockport War Memorial Committee.

1940s

Keep Calm and Carry On Painting

Fig 61: War Memorial Art Gallery with Stockport Technical School behind (circa 1945).

Unlike other local societies, which either closed or were struggling to remain operational during World War II, Stockport Art Guild remained healthily active. The conflict made life more difficult but the Guild were determined to continue holding their weekly sessions in the Life Room of the School of Art at Stockport College and the Annual Exhibition at the War Memorial Art Gallery.

At the Guild's Annual General Meeting on February 3rd 1940, Chairman Scott:

> "Congratulated the Guild on having put up a show of work in the recent 20th Exhibition, which, in spite of war conditions, had maintained both quality and numbers. He considered that the invitation extended to Red Rose Guild members to exhibit craftwork had been repaid by the increased craftwork exhibition and by the many extra visitors this had brought to the gallery."

During the early 1940s, membership levels were still low with only: 45 Pictorial, 5 Craft (7 classed as joint) and 4 Associate Members. Members serving with the forces were excused their subscription fees. In the minutes of a meeting during this time it was noted that 'it was agreed that an attempt will be made to carry out our winter programme, in spite of the blackout.' The only detrimental consequence of the conflict appeared to be that the Annual Exhibition catalogue booklet was downgraded to a leaflet due to paper shortages.

The Manchester Guardian picked out Marjorie Mort's new series of genre studies in the Guild's Annual Exhibition of 1940, saying:

> "The best of them, 'Second House' is a particularly fine piece of work. Miss Mort also proves that she is equally at home in the more familiar landscape even though she finds her inspiration in the red brick of factory walls, the sweep of a canal, and the red metal of an iron bridge."

At the AGM in 1941, the President remarked that:

> "Mr Tom Scott recalled the hopes expressed at the last Annual General Meeting, that another year would bring a brighter outlook. Instead, it seemed

that the shadow of war was now deeper, but we should be wise to continue in our faith that there were better things ahead, and in the meantime to carry on with the Guild activities and with the interests of daily life. These activities and interests helped keep us sane and fit for the War work which must be done."

At the beginning of 1943, Stockport Art Guild introduced 'Life Membership' which they awarded to people who they felt had made a great contribution to the Guild. At the AGM on the 20th February that year, James Chettle was the first person to be bestowed with this honour. He exhibited a painting at the 1943 Annual Exhibition called "Above the Valley." It was recently included in a 2011-12 exhibition of landscape paintings at the Stockport War Memorial Gallery called 'This Green and Pleasant Land' - the painting was back on the walls of the gallery, some 68 years after it was first exhibited.

Fig 62: 'Above the Valley' by James Chettle (1943).

By the 1944 AGM, the Stockport Guild was already starting to think about post-war development. A 'Ways and Means Committee' was formed to review all activity, including the Guild's financial health, and make recommendations for any changes or new ideas once the war was over. There was also a call for Stockport Art Guild to raise its profile amongst the local community. Mr Mostyn made an appeal for wider and more varied publicity, arguing that the Guild could make the town of Stockport more conscious of their activity.

Wilfred Colclough wrote a comment on the Chairman's AGM address in the 1944 minute book, saying:

> *"The chairman noted the increased activities of the Guild during the previous year which he felt was creditable especially under war conditions. Under such circumstances small cultural groups were threatened with extinction. That had not been the lot of the Stockport Art Guild, whose membership had increased."*

Colclough proposed that they start to think about the Stockport Guild as an 'Arts' Club rather than an 'Art' Club to encourage Literature, Music and Dancing, as well as Drawing and Painting. He felt that there should be a close liaison between all the art forms and a need to draw into close contact artists, writers and musicians. He said that they should be aiming for 'a culture studio with facilities for lectures.' This was seen by some of the membership as having the consequence of attempting to build bridges with the 'decorative artists' once again.

The Stockport Guild saw themselves being swept up in the excitement of a brand new wartime BBC Radio series in 1944 called 'The Brains Trust'. The format of this popular Sunday afternoon programme was that members of the public would send in questions that a series of expert panellists had to answer. The Stockport Guild Council wrote to the series producers and offered up James Chettle and John Sandiford to be their art experts for the panel. Maybe they had been inspired by Harry Rutherford's stint on the BBC show Cabaret Cartoons a few years earlier. There is no record of whether either of them actually appeared on the show.

Fig 63: 'Wester Ross Highlands' by Wilfred Colclough (1958).

Chettle exhibited with Stockport Art Guild for the last time in 1944. Tom Scott announced to the membership that the Guild had suffered a great loss; Mr Chettle had died in December at the age of 73. He went on to give the following eulogy:

"The north has lost a painter of real merit and of very individual outlook in the practice of his art. He was a sincere lover of the quieter and more serene moods of nature, and one always looked for, and invariably found, a serenity, which both convinced and captivated all those who had ever felt the emotional values he so ably painted. In his choice of subject, Mr Chettle never sought the sensational, and because of that his colour and technique was such as could readily be both appreciated and understood. He was for so many years a member of the Stockport Art Guild, and he was unfailing in his support of the annual exhibitions to which he always sent a number of paintings. Not only for this will he be missed, for he was always ready to give to individual members a candid and constructive criticism, based upon his wide experience as a painter."

By the end of Chettle's life, there were no art societies in the area that had not had his support of one kind or another. As well as his time on the War Memorial Art Gallery Committee he had also been: President of the Royal Manchester Institution; President of the Athenaeum Graphic Club; President of the Manchester Academy and President of the Stockport Art Guild.

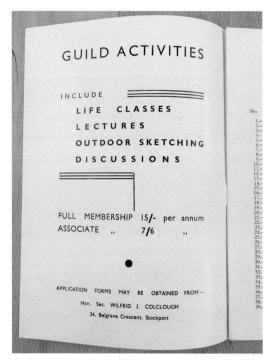

Fig 64: 1946 Annual Exhibition catalogue 'advert'.

New Beginnings

By the end of the war, Wilfred Colclough had settled into his role as SAG's Honorary Secretary and had injected a newfound sense of energy and lots of fresh ideas. One of them was a new 'portfolio scheme' that involved the creation of three folios full of the best examples of artwork from across the membership. These showcases would then be passed around the local area, promoting membership of the Guild and showing the high standard of work produced. Although this scheme proved very popular, it also became instantly problematic and within a year all the portfolios had gone missing whilst on their travels.

In 1946, the Guild's Annual Exhibition in the War Memorial Gallery was made up 160 exhibits. The main space upstairs hosted an impressive display of oil paintings including work by Walter Potts, Alfred Blackman and a new member called John D. Howard. Discussing the paintings that had been accepted into the 27th Annual Exhibition that year Colclough added:

> *"A democratically-elected selection committee vets them (the entries) and this year rejected about thirty. One of the biggest difficulties is allocating wall space so that one picture does not 'kill' another."*

Colclough was determined to carry on promoting the Stockport Guild and started an advertising campaign in 1946 to drive up membership. That year, a message inside their Annual Exhibition catalogue also invited people to come along to a 'criticism of rejected works' that was going to be led by Colclough.

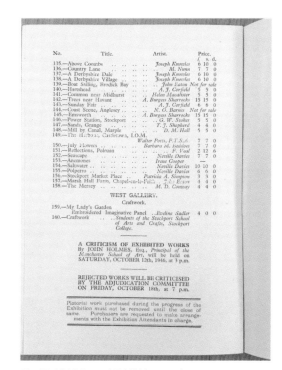

Fig 65: 1946 Annual Exhibition catalogue – 'rejected works' invitation.

A New Home

In March 1947, Alfred Blackman took over as Chairman and President, and Stockport Art Guild continued to see more developments come out of the Ways and Means Committee. One of the most significant changes was the decision to start renting a large room and annex space, at the studio above Hidderley's wallpaper emporium at No. 4 St Peter's Square in the centre of Stockport.

A 'House Committee' was formed to deal with the cleaning and decoration of the studio and there was an appeal for furniture to fill the space. Members donated several easels, chairs, crockery and an armchair. They also set up a reference library of art books and everyone was encouraged to lend books for a limited time. Popular periodicals of the time such as "The Studio," "Expression" and "The Artist" were also purchased and made available for members to read.

By the beginning of August 1947 the studio was up and running for members to use. It immediately proved to be a popular space and before long SAG membership had doubled. Life classes were held there every Friday evening from 7-9pm for a fee of 6d per person. Still life classes were held there occasionally on Wednesdays as an alternative to the life evening. Everyone was invited, for a fee of 1/- per day, to use the new studio at anytime. It was brought to their attention that 'we have facilities in the studio for making tea, but at present no supply of tea, sugar or milk. Please bring these with you if you wish to enjoy a drink.'

From the outset, the fine artists seemed to outnumber the decorative arts in the studio space and as a result the craft side of the Guild waned once again.

The Ways and Means Committee also introduced a full programme of events at the new studio and they began trialling a series of member quiz nights and lectures on the first Thursday of each month. The BBC Radio programme 'The Brains Trust' was hugely popular and so the Art Guild held their own quiz "An Art Brains Trust" on Thursday 6th November 1947. Tom Scott, John Davies, Wilfred Colclough and George Stokes (who had become a MAFA Member by then) acted as the panel of 'Brains' and Alfred Blackman took the role of question master.

Fig 66: John Davies sketching en plein air.

At the same time as the Guild was settling into their new studio space, there was a renewed desire by the Education Committee to maximise the use of the War Memorial Building. Alderman Patten reminded the Corporation of Stockport in 1947 that despite it being a sacred place of remembrance it was far too underused. The building was now 22 years old and, despite its position at the heart of the town, was largely unknown to the younger generations of Stopfordians.

Fig 67: 'Malcesine' by John Davies.

In Tom Scott's final AGM address before he retired from the Guild Council that year he said:

> *"...the standard of work continued to improve, but he would like to see an increase in dimensions of works for the upper gallery, in order to achieve a sense of greater importance."*

SAG's Annual Exhibition at the War Memorial Gallery at the end of 1947 included a couple of paintings, 'Rhododendrons' and 'The Gower Coast,' by GH James who had died earlier that year. Wilfred Colclough delivered a lecture at the studio that December entitled "The Nature of Art and its relationship to Society." The invitation to the talk read 'The speaker whose ideas on Art have been influenced by the writings of the Russian Philosopher, Leo Tolstoy, will attempt to define Art. The vexed question

STOCKPORT ART GUILD

1st November, 1947

STUDIO ARRANGEMENTS

LIFE CLASSES   These will be held each Wednesday and Friday at 7 p.m.
starting on Wednesday 5th November, bring your own Easel and
stool. Class Fee 6d per night.

STILL LIFE CLASS   This will be arranged as an alternative to the Life Class
on Wednesday Evenings. Fee 6d.

LECTURES, ETC.   The First Thursday of each month will be a Lecture night,
to which Friends will be most welcome. The arrangements
for November and December are as follows:-

THURDAY   "An Art Brains Trust"
6th Nov.   Brains. Messrs. Scott, Davies, Colclough, Stokes.
Question Master Mr. Blackman.

THURSDAY   "The Nature of Art and its relationship to Society"
4th Dec.   Speaker. W. J. Colclough.
The Speaker whose ideas on Art have been
influenced by the writings of the Russian
Philosopher, Leo Tolstoy, will attempt to
define Art. The vexed question of Art and
morality will be discussed and the Social
significance of the Artist and his work will
be examined.

USE OF STUDIO BY   The Council wishes to encourage the use of the studio at
INDIVIDUAL MEMBERS   times other than those devoted to Group Activities. Members
who wish to use the Studio will be charged a fee of 1/- per
day. Application for the Studio key should be made a
Council Members (For further details see Studio notice board)

NOTICE TO ASSOCIATE MEMBERS   On Thursday 20th November at 7 p.m. the
APPLICATIONS FOR FULL MEMBERSHIP   Guild Council will meet in the Studio to
consider applications for full membership.
Applicants should inform the Secretary of their intention before Thursday,
13th November, and present at least three framed works for the Council's
consideration - on 20th November (Thursday)

REFRESHMENT   We have facilities in the Studio for making Tea, but
at present no supply of Tea, sugar or milk.
Bring these with you if you wish to enjoy a drink.

GIFTS AND DONATIONS   The Council wishes to thank all those members who have
responded to the appeal for furniture, etc. we have
several chairs promised, one arm chair, several easels.
A projector for lantern slides, for the latter we need a screen. Can anyone
help? More crocks are needed.

LIBRARY   It is planned to form a reference library of Art Books
to be housed in the Studio. Will members who would be
willing to lend books for a limited period to the
Reference Library, please inform the Secretary.

PERIODICALS   Copies of "The Artist" "The Studio" and "Expression"
will be purchased.

SPECIAL NOTICE

28th   Annual   Exhibition

As the War Memorial Gallery will be used for a Public Service on
9th November, all Pictures MUST be removed before 7th November, (Friday)

Fig 68: Notice of Studio Arrangements - Nov 1947.

of morality will be discussed and the social significance of the Artist and his work will be examined.'

By the end of the decade Colclough, with the support of John Howard, was continuing to modernize Stockport Art Guild and introduce new ideas. Hal Yates, another progressive artist and Manchester Academician, became a member around this time.

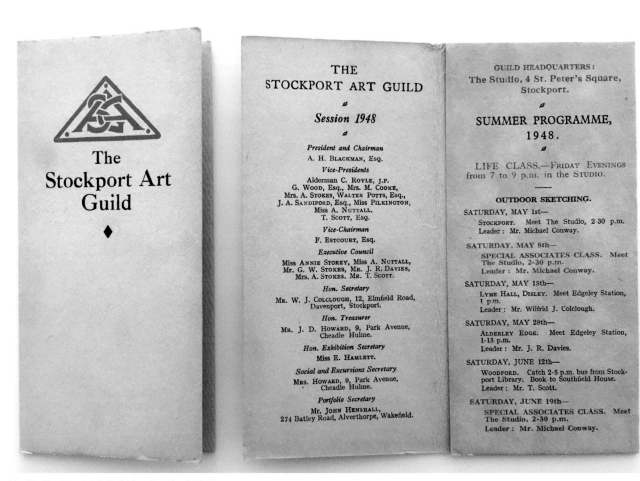

Fig 69: Stockport Art Guild Session Card 1948.

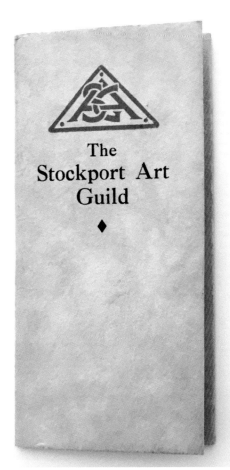

The Stockport Art Guild

♦

THE STOCKPORT ART GUILD

Session 1949

President and Chairman
J. R. DAVIES, ESQ.

Vice-Presidents
ALDERMAN C. ROYLE,
DR. E. GWYN THOMAS,
G. WOOD, ESQ., P. O'BRIEN, ESQ.,
MRS. STOKES, MR. SANDIFORD,
WALTER POTTS, ESQ., MISS NUTTALL,
T. SCOTT, ESQ., MISS STOREY,
MISS HAMLETT, MISS PILKINGTON.

Vice-Chairman
A. H. BLACKMAN, ESQ.

Guild Council
MISS NUTTALL, MR. T. SCOTT, MR. STANLEY,
MR. STOKES, MRS. STOKES, MISS GOULDING,
MR. WRYCROFT, MR. JONES,
MRS. HOWARD (Associate Representative).

Hon. Secretary
MR. W. J. COLCLOUGH, 24, Valley Road,
Bramhall.

Hon. Treasurer
MR. J. HOWARD, 9, Park Avenue,
Cheadle Hulme.

Hon. Portfolio Secretary
MR. J. HENSHALL, 274, Batley Road,
Alverthorpe, Wakefield.

Hon. Social Secretary
MRS. MORLEY, 13, Woodsmoor Lane,
Stockport.

Adjudication and Hanging Committee
MESSRS. BLACKMAN, SCOTT, STANLEY, HENSHALL,
POTTS, MISS BOULTON.

GUILD HEADQUARTERS:
The Studio, 4 St. Peter's Square,
Stockport.

SUMMER PROGRAMME, 1949.

LIFE CLASS,
WEDNESDAY AND FRIDAY EVENINGS
from 7 to 9 p.m.

ASSOCIATES CLASS,
MONDAY EVENINGS from 7 to 9 p.m.

OUTDOOR SKETCHING.

SATURDAY, APRIL 30th—
STOCKPORT. Meet The Studio, 2-30 p.m.
Leader: Mr. Ainsworth.

SATURDAY, MAY 7th—
BRAMALL HALL. Meet Park Gates, 2-30 p.m.
Leader: Mrs. Howard.

SATURDAY, MAY 21st—
FLETCHER MOSS GALLERY, DIDSBURY. Meet
Mersey Square, 2 p.m.
Leader: Mr. W. J. Colclough.

SATURDAY, JUNE 4th—
ALDERLEY EDGE. Meet Edgeley Station,
1 p.m.
Leader: Mr. Stokes.

SATURDAY, JUNE 18th—
LYME PARK, DISLEY. Meet Edgeley Station,
1 p.m.
Leader: Mr. Ainsworth.

Fig 70: Stockport Art Guild Session Card 1949.

Hal Yates

Hal Yates (1907-1979) joined Manchester Academy of Fine Arts and Stockport Art Guild in 1949. By that time he was in his late thirties and becoming well-known for his confidently handled watercolour scenes.

He exhibited his paintings in a large number of galleries and exhibitions, including: the Royal Academy; the Royal Institute of Painters in Water Colours (where he was elected a member); MAFA and SAG.

He exhibited three paintings entitled 'Harbour Installations,' 'Poeticus' and 'Severn at Newtown' in the Stockport Art Guild's 30th Annual Exhibition at the War Memorial Gallery. In 1957 he displayed six watercolours in the Lancashire Group of Artists 5th Annual Exhibition at the gallery. His work is currently held in the public collections of Manchester City Art Gallery, Salford Art Gallery and Stockport Heritage Services.

Yates remained an amateur artist throughout his life and spent his career in the family firm of seed merchants in Manchester, eventually becoming Chairman.

Fig 71: Hal Yates at his easel en plein air (circa 1957).

At the 1949 AGM, in reconciliatory mood, John Howard raised the point that Stockport Art Guild appeared to offer very little to its Decorative Art members and as a result has 'caused the inevitable decline of that section of the Guild.' He felt deeply disturbed about this and called for a fuller discussion over the question of what the Guild could offer crafters. Shortly afterwards, craft members Miss Hamlett and Miss Storey were approached 'to see if the ladies could revive craft interest.' However, nothing substantial could be done.

At the same meeting, Colclough said that he:

> *"had been profoundly disturbed at the method of adjudication in the past..... non-academic work had been refused, so that the non-catholic taste of the adjudication committee was in evidence."*

He proposed a motion for an amendment to one of the rules in the Guild's constitution that: 'one work may be nominated by the member for exhibition' thus ensuring that at least one work, however unconventional, from each member would be displayed.

He felt strongly that exhibition selection should be accountable and that every member should have some degree of say in the matter of the type of art to be displayed. After a lively discussion, a vote was taken and the resolution was passed 23 for / 7 against.

Throughout the final year of the decade, the studio in St Peter's Square increased in popularity. There was an Associates Class on Monday evenings and Life Classes every Wednesday and Friday evening. Executive Council meetings were now also being held there, as well as other Guild events and artist talks. That year, one-man shows in the studio included John Davies (9th July), George Stokes (6th August), John Howard (27th August) and Wilfred Colclough (24th September) – and there was a growing waiting list of other members who wanted to exhibit. At the Council meeting on 7th September 1949 it was agreed that solo shows by non-members would also be accepted at a cost of 2/10/- per week.

The Manchester Guardian used Wilfred Colclough's show to comment on the town's art scene, declaring:

> "Stockport is growing steadily more interested in painting and is freeing itself from the 'shadow of Manchester' according to Dr Gwyn Thomas who opened a Stockport Art Guild exhibition at the St Peter's Square studio on Saturday. The Art Guild has its third one-man show; here are 40 odd paintings by Wilfred Colclough, the best of which bring out his talent for clean, expressive colour."

The Guild was in good shape…or was it?

Fig 72: George Stokes sketching en plein air.

The

1950s

Hard times at the Guild

Fig 73: Albert Sewter, head of Fine Arts at Manchester University (left), John Chirnside (centre), and John Davies, President of the Stockport Art Guild, analyse a self-portrait by John Chirnside (1952).

The decade started with a financial crisis for Stockport Art Guild under the Presidency of John Davies. At the Annual General Meeting in March 1950, their auditor, Mr Sylvester, announced that they had a credit balance of just £20.17.1 ½, against which there were bills owing of £30.12.10. The Guild was in debt.

A debate then followed as to whether they could continue to afford the studio annex space at St Peter's Square. It was decided by a vote of fourteen to twelve that, provided financial guarantors were forthcoming, Stockport Guild would continue to occupy the studio annex until at least the September Quarter Day 1950.

Mr Sylvester made a number of suggestions as to how they could raise funds. These included inviting wealthy locals to become patrons of SAG; holding a fundraising dance at Stockport Town Hall and offering more time for one-man exhibitions at their studio. It was also agreed that the annual subscription would be raised, although this was not without some resistance, as John Howard believed the motion to raise subscriptions was out of order as 'no previous notice of the change had been given' and suggested making the increase voluntary. He was overruled and it was decided to increase membership fees.

Immediately after the Annual General Meeting, Walter Potts planned a solo show of fifty of his paintings for the Guild's Studio in September. Harry Rutherford attended the exhibition opening and was happy to have been invited. Harry's older brother George, on the other hand, wasn't so keen and wrote in a letter to Harry:

> "I have been invited to go to Stockport to see a one man show of the work of Walter Potts, could anything be more unutterably utter? Even great art delighteth me not, so what of Potkin?"

Although Potts's exhibition was very successful and resulted in a £6 commission to the Guild, it was agreed that an Extraordinary General Meeting was to be held to decide the fate of the studio annex. At the EGM on 7th December 1950, President Davies announced to the membership that it was now financially impossible to keep the studio annex space and not to end up in great debt. He explained that 'strenuous efforts had been made to keep the space but now the Guild Council reluctantly felt that the time has come for the annex to be given up.' The motion was passed unanimously to inform the landlord, Mr Hadden Ley, that they were going to relinquish the tenancy of the annex space from March 25th 1951.

Fig 74: The Mayor of Stockport viewing Stockport Art Guild's Annual Exhibition (circa 1950s).

John Chirnside

John Chirnside was an enthusiastic amateur painter who joined SAG in the early Fifties. He was a lecturer in textile design at Manchester College of Technology for almost over forty years until his retirement in 1978.

Manchester had become an industrial powerhouse thanks to the cotton revolution of the mid-nineteenth century and the textile businesses that followed in the twentieth century like the one that James Chettle built up. It is, therefore, hardly surprising that, as a Mancunian and an artist, Chirnside became a leading academic on the subject of textile design. In 1938 he published a Journal claiming that artists working freelance in textile design were the only significant creative force in textile design:

'Many modem painters have designed textiles and we may say that whatever evidence exists of a new and contemporary style in modem fabrics is due to the experiments of present day painters and sculptors."

Chirnside's artistic status moved up a gear by the end of the 1950s. He became a member of the Manchester Academy of Fine Arts in 1958 and in 1959 he was elected as Stockport Art Guild's President and Chairman. For the next twenty years he split his time between lecturing at the College of Technology (which later became UMIST) and portrait painting at SAG and MAFA. He died in 1995.

In 1952, Chirnside was asked to deliver the opening address at Stockport Guild's 33rd Annual Exhibition. He didn't hold back:

"Far too many art galleries are repellent places - Ugh! The smell of cooking cabbage that always seems to linger around them, it's no wonder it's an awful job getting people inside them... but the Stockport War Memorial Gallery is one of the nicest."

Albert Sewter, head of Fine Arts at Manchester University, formally opened the show that year. He replied by saying:

"It would be difficult and expensive to make 'repellent' galleries look attractive, and besides, most paintings are meant to be hung in homes."

"Stockport is one of the towns most in need of an infusion of artistic feeling and ideas. There are places where no artists live, and where no exhibitions are held. Stockport is not as bad as that. It is at least aware of the existence of art and its aims."

Sewter added that he thought it was a 'disgrace to the town' that when he had visited SAG's exhibition the previous year he had noticed that not one piece of artwork had been sold. Immediately after his speech the attending crowd apparently re-examined all the work in the gallery with added interest, many noting down prices and discussing purchasing one or two.

Rule Changes

In the early 1950s, the Guild updated their rules to state that 'there shall be two classes of member: Full and Associate. Entry to the Guild shall be by way of the latter class.' Election Day took place once a year. Associate Members needed to present between three and six original works, framed for adjudication. If they were successful, they would immediately be promoted to Full Membership (on payment of the higher fees). Anyone who didn't get through the adjudication was allowed to apply the following year.

In addition to 'Full' and 'Associate' members, there was also an 'Honorary' Members class who were elected at the AGM in recognition of exceptional service to the Guild. Honorary Members didn't need to pay an annual subscription to be part of the Guild but had the same privileges as a Full Member.

The John Howard Years

At the 1953 Annual General Meeting, Chairman John Davies and Honorary Secretary Wilfred Colclough retired from their posts on the Guild Council. Mr Colclough commented that he had only taken the position reluctantly and had ended up remaining in the post for ten years. John Howard was elected as Stockport Guild's new Chairman.

Associates night was on Mondays; Wednesdays were exclusively for Full Members (with a professional model) and Friday evenings were for both classes, with Associate Members volunteering to sit in as the portrait model.

As the fifties advanced, so did John Howard and John Chirnside's involvement in the weekly sessions. They both began assisting Associate Members on Monday nights and also introduced an occasional element at the end of the Monday class where members would pin up the drawings they had done and one or two Full Members would attend and constructively criticize the work. This initiative was very popular and became known as the 'Pin up and Criticism' session.

Stockport Art Guild's Annual Exhibition was the most popular show at the War Memorial Art Gallery in 1954. With an average attendance of over 1,200 people a week, it smashed the visitor numbers (<300 pw) who went to see the touring Royal Academy show at the gallery earlier that year.

By the mid-fifties the Guild's recruitment advertising campaign was in full flow. They were regularly placing ads in The Artist Magazine announcing 'Painting: Monday, Wednesday and Friday evenings. Alternate Saturdays: Outside Sketching.' And their Annual Exhibition catalogue stated that 'Membership of the Stockport Art Guild should be of value to all interested in painting and the appreciation of art. Activities include: Life classes, lectures, discussions, demonstrations etc.' By this time, Full Membership cost 17/6 and Associate Membership was 12/6.

It is interesting to note how much the taste for urban landscapes had changed over a quarter of a century. In 1930 The Manchester Guardian saw the Stockport vista as a typical grubby industrial town, however by 1956 they felt that:

> *"Stockport and its neighbourhood is probably the most paintable area in the North West. Its buildings compose themselves in unending shifts of level and plane: the hard Derbyshire countryside at its edges runs into a rich, huddled, grey vitality at its heart, like a vast industrial St Ives."*

Fig 75: The Stockport Art Guild Annual Exhibition (circa 1950s).

St Ives School artists such as Alfred Wallis, Alan Davie and Sir Terry Frost had fuelled the post-war popularity of Abstract Expressionism and the desire to explore boundaries between representation and abstraction. The Stockport Guild, with its roots in the Arts and Crafts Movement, had always focused on representational art. However, a debate over non-representational art dominated the 1957 Annual General Meeting. John Howard said in his President's address:

> *"The Guild is a club interested primarily in the practice of painting. We are not tied to any particular 'ism' or outlook. We do not teach. Our members learn by association with other members and are completely free to develop as they wish."*

There was a strong show of hands at the meeting to support a series of new sessions on Tuesdays or Saturdays for an experimental group of members to paint in a non-representational manner. The motion was passed that the Guild would trial 'Modern Art' for the coming winter Season and that Mr Runcie and Mr Stott would start off by giving a talk on 'an approach to non-figurative art.'

The Guild was entering a new era....

1960s

The Three Johns

Fig 76: Harry Rutherford judging members' work (circa 1961).

The sixties was a decade of tremendous change, not only in popular culture but also in fine art. Pop Art had emerged as a reaction against Abstract Expressionism. Sir Antony Caro was creating exciting Modernist sculptures; Colour Field painting was gaining popularity and David Hockney was producing some of his most seminal work.

In Stockport, the Borough Council had started holding their own annual Open Exhibition at the War Memorial Gallery and it was gaining popularity. They said that the Stockport Open was designed to give local artists, 'not members of recognised societies or arts clubs,' an opportunity to show their work publicly. This was clearly a reference to the allegedly closed shop elitism of SAG's membership policy.

By the start of the 1960s, John Chirnside had taken over from John Howard as President and Chairman. Despite a record number of new Associate Members enrolling in the Guild, attendance at the Monday night Associates Evening had declined drastically. It was therefore agreed that the Monday night sessions would be open to all members and be devoted to painting still life subjects.

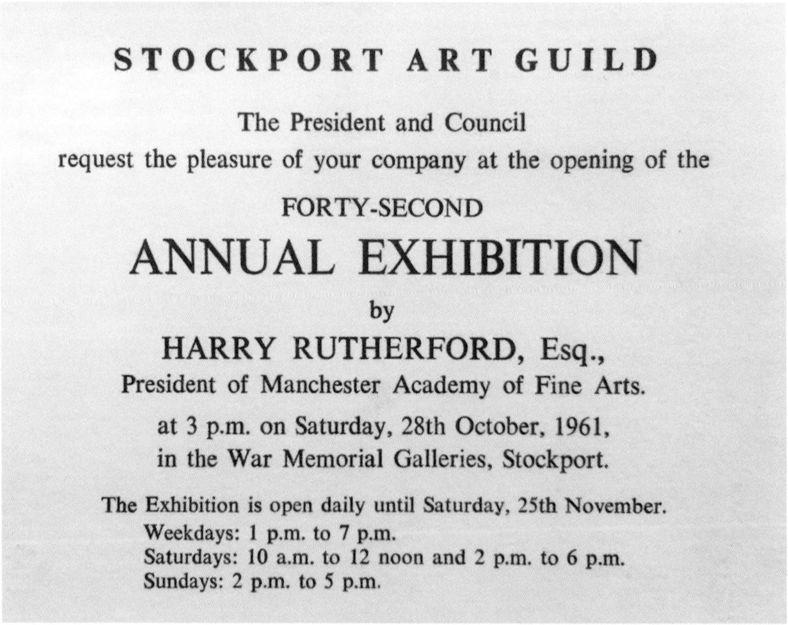

STOCKPORT ART GUILD

The President and Council
request the pleasure of your company at the opening of the

FORTY-SECOND

ANNUAL EXHIBITION

by

HARRY RUTHERFORD, Esq.,
President of Manchester Academy of Fine Arts.

at 3 p.m. on Saturday, 28th October, 1961,
in the War Memorial Galleries, Stockport.

The Exhibition is open daily until Saturday, 25th November.
Weekdays: 1 p.m. to 7 p.m.
Saturdays: 10 a.m. to 12 noon and 2 p.m. to 6 p.m.
Sundays: 2 p.m. to 5 p.m.

Fig 77: The 42nd Annual Exhibition (1961), opened by Harry Rutherford.

Harry Rutherford opened the Guild's 42nd Annual Exhibition in 1961. He was a well-known TV personality by now and had also just been elected as the President of the Manchester Academy of Fine Arts. Chirnside saw this a fantastic opportunity to confirm the superior status of the Guild's exhibition over the Stockport Open and also to publicise an Honorary Member of SAG who had gone on to achieve a highly distinguished career.

Fig 78: Harry Rutherford and Hal Yates (circa 1961).

Bigger and Better

The 1962 Annual Exhibition was held at the War Memorial Gallery from the 27th October to 24th November 1962. At the opening, John Chirnside reiterated the status of the SAG show by proudly informing more than 150 people packed into the main Upper Gallery:

> "The exhibition is larger than ever. More people entered, and they entered better pictures. People are becoming more and more interested in pictures, and the fact that this exhibition is so well-attended today gives a clear picture of this association. I hope it gives a picture of a lively, healthy and growing association. In these unsettled times it is a good thing to belong to some association based on the more permanent values of life."

Stockport Art Guild was in bullish mood and stood well in comparison to two prestigious exhibitions in the gallery in 1962. An exhibition of early paintings and drawings by LS Lowry RA (from the collection of the Rev. Geoffrey Bennett) ran from the 15th September to the 13th October. The Guild's exhibition immediately followed the Lowry show. Then there was the Royal Academy's Touring Exhibition that ran from 8th December until the 5th January 1963.

Weekly attendance figures for the three exhibitions showed Lowry's show had 469 visitors; the Guild's exhibition had 357 and the RA show only had 72 visitors. Chirnside had every right to be proud.

The weekly sessions for 1963 were still being held in the Guild's studio in St Peter's Square with painting evenings continuing to be on Mondays, Wednesdays and Fridays.

That year the summer outdoor sketching programme included trips to: Marple Dale, led by watercolourist Frank Escourt; Millers Dale, led by John Howard and Fletcher Moss in Didsbury, led by John Chirnside. The winter programme featured a demonstration of Flower Painting by John Churnside; a lecture by Hal Yates and a lecture and demonstration by John Howard entitled 'A practical approach to painting.'

The third John, Mr John Hall, joined the Guild at the end of 1963.

At the AGM early in 1964, John Chirnside said that he felt that their recent Annual Exhibition of four hundred works "...was indicative of the type of artwork we, as a Guild, liked – good sound painting, representational rather than abstract of varied subject matter."

The seismic shifts happening in popular culture had yet to make any real impact on the outlook of the Stockport Art Guild.

Fig 79: John Chirnside demonstrates flower painting at a Guild meeting in 1963.

There was positive news at the meeting when the Guild's Honorary Secretary, Anne Ramscar, reported that forty-two new members had joined SAG during the previous twelve months, bringing the membership to 184. This was made up of: 68 Full, 108 Associate and 8 Honorary Members.

In August 1964, John Howard negotiated a discount scheme with Derek and Sheila Jennings, the then owners of Stockport's oldest art suppliers, Turners, for Guild members to get up to 10% off their art materials. Fifty four years later, Turners Art Shop is still trading and continues to support SAG members in the same way.

By the mid 1960s, SAG membership had reached an all time high of 218 members and the Guild Council were concerned that their annual exhibition wouldn't be able to accommodate all the members' work. John Chirnside informed the membership at the following AGM that in future there would be more severe judgement on all artwork submitted to the Annual Exhibition and as a result pictures would be less easily accepted. Rule 4 was also amended to reduce the maximum number of pictures that each member could submit from 12 to 8 pieces.

At the same Annual General Meeting, Chirnside also spoke about the pleasant and happy atmosphere that prevailed in the Studio:

> *"As artists we work well together – we can also be sociable together, as witnessed at our January party. We welcome new members but we have no need to go out of our way to look for them. We have a comfortable balance in the bank and need not work on a shoestring. In all, it's a very satisfactory state of affairs."*

A Pickwickian Club

In December 1966, Richard Hemingway, a journalist for the Stockport Express, wrote an article in the newspaper describing a scene he saw in The Stockport Arms on St. Petersgate:

> *"The small group of men who walked into the bar intrigued me with a certain air as though they belonged to some Pickwickian Club. I learned from my companion that they were painters. They had just spent an evening in their studio in St Peter's Square sketching. Custom dictated that they round off the evening with a drink at the local."*

He went on to describe the visit that he made to the Guild's St Peter's Square Studio:

> *"Beyond the front door stretched a long flight of stairs. The attic studio was typical of any artist's workshop. The walls seemed bare, easels were propped against the walls and, on the plain boards, three electric fires did their best*

to take the chill off the air. In the centre of the room was the stand on which the model was to pose. It was made up of odd boxes, a ladder and a backrest, all covered with drapes of material to obscure the peculiar framework, which made the shape that they wanted. Here they work in nearly all mediums of painting and drawing."

Sadly, not all reviews were to be as positive and open-minded. Only a month earlier, another journalist at the Stockport Express gave Stockport Guild's Annual Exhibition a scathing review, describing it as 'not the sort of show to pull in the crowds.'

The journalist, writing only under the initials 'KD', went on to say that:

"A group of elderly spinsters meeting in Basingstoke to discuss crochet work in the Age of Queen Ann would not have cause to raise an eyelid at the annual exhibition of paintings presented by Stockport Art Guild.

How long the people of Stockport can put up with the quite ludicrous situation which makes this town barren of music and barren of any painting post-dating the Industrial Revolution has long been a question over which I have furrowed my brow.

The sheer, well-meaning futility of it all is summed up in this present exhibition. It will remain in the Memorial Gallery unlooked at by all save the painters who produced it, a few casual passers-by seeking shelter from the rain, and myself, who am paid for writing of it.

Undoubtedly these paintings could give a lot of pleasure to well-meaning artistic illiterates. But to have them – and other much worse than them in the permanent collection – as almost the sole concession which this Borough makes to activities other than the intestinal and soporific, is a matter for ribald laughter and self-immolation on the steps of the Town Hall.

The good artistic sense of the public can be judged by the fact that only a few of them ever set foot in the War Memorial Gallery."

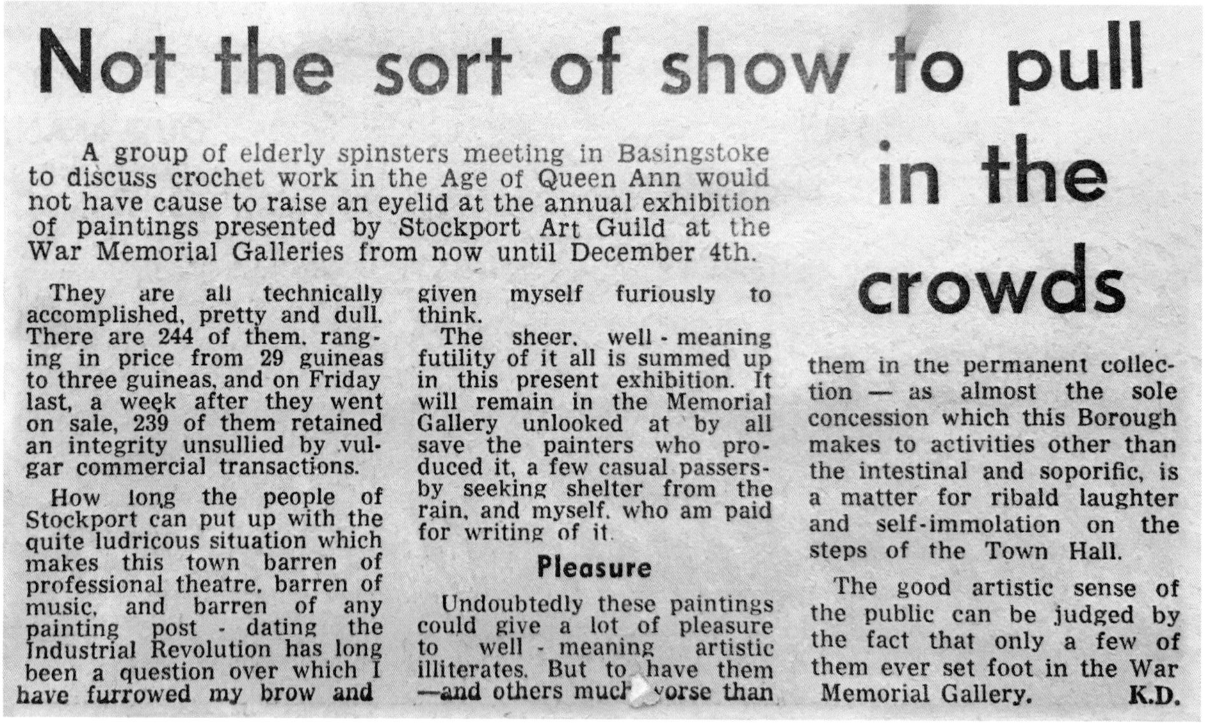

Not the sort of show to pull in the crowds

A group of elderly spinsters meeting in Basingstoke to discuss crochet work in the Age of Queen Ann would not have cause to raise an eyelid at the annual exhibition of paintings presented by Stockport Art Guild at the War Memorial Galleries from now until December 4th.

They are all technically accomplished, pretty and dull. There are 244 of them, ranging in price from 29 guineas to three guineas, and on Friday last, a week after they went on sale, 239 of them retained an integrity unsullied by vulgar commercial transactions.

How long the people of Stockport can put up with the quite ludicrous situation which makes this town barren of professional theatre, barren of music, and barren of any painting post - dating the Industrial Revolution has long been a question over which I have furrowed my brow and given myself furiously to think.

The sheer, well - meaning futility of it all is summed up in this present exhibition. It will remain in the Memorial Gallery unlooked at by all save the painters who produced it, a few casual passers-by seeking shelter from the rain, and myself, who am paid for writing of it.

Pleasure

Undoubtedly these paintings could give a lot of pleasure to well - meaning artistic illiterates. But to have them —and others much worse than them in the permanent collection — as almost the sole concession which this Borough makes to activities other than the intestinal and soporific, is a matter for ribald laughter and self-immolation on the steps of the Town Hall.

The good artistic sense of the public can be judged by the fact that only a few of them ever set foot in the War Memorial Gallery.　　**K.D.**

Fig 80: A scathing review of Stockport Art Guild's 1966 Annual Exhibition.

By 1967, studio attendance levels, especially on Mondays, Tuesdays and Wednesday nights, declined again and there was a growing feeling in the Council that members were not getting as much as they could from their membership.

Anecdotal feedback was that some of the more experienced painters found the set ups uninteresting on the still life evenings. Other members found the 7pm start too early and one of the women said she would benefit from more help from Full Members. John Chirnside questioned whether the Guild needed a mid-week life class at all. One of the members, Mr Jackson, suggested changing the theme of sessions each month, so that there would be a nude model for a month, followed by a costume model for four weeks, then still life and so on.

It was agreed that a new style Associates Evening would be trialled on Mondays.

The sessions were to start later, at 7.15pm, and a rota was set up for artists to take it in turns to bring along and set up their own still life compositions. Full Members also arranged to come along from time to time to offer help to any Associates who needed it.

John Chirnside, frustrated by the falling studio attendances, said that the Guild was not in a position to give tuition and recommended that members started 'painting in groups.' He added:

> *"Some members joined us solely to exhibit – they were welcome and their work enriched the exhibition – others came to lectures and criticism, while yet another group came to the studio two or three times a week to use the facilities provided – to the mutual benefit of all. It was up to ourselves – so long as we paid our subs, we could do as we pleased – paint as we pleased – 'dribble' if we liked, but we wouldn't like to say that such pictures had the same chance of getting into the exhibition!"*

Discussions around the problem of dwindling attendances continued to dominate Guild Council meetings. Mr LJ Bowker expressed concern at the falling off of the Friday evening attendances and Bill Bartram, the Honorary Secretary at the time, was asked to contact the Students' Union at the Stockport College of Further Education with a view to obtaining models at 7/6 an hour.

Unfortunately, within six months, the new format Associates Evening on Mondays had not improved attendance and so the classes were suspended due to lack of support. Tuesday night numbers were also too spasmodic to cover the cost of the professional models, so these were suspended too.

Christine Garner, now aged 74, joined the Guild as an Associate Member in the late sixties. She recalls:

> *"I used to go on a Monday night for portrait painting, I enjoyed it, the atmosphere was friendly and inviting. The "three Johns" were there – Messrs Chirnside, Hall and Howard.*

I didn't know what to expect on my first visit but after watching John Chirnside painting with soft pastels I went and sat next to him so my love of pastelling began. John was brilliant and he gave many demonstrations of portrait painting to the Guild - we were very lucky to have him.

The Guild used to hold critic nights, I'm not sure whether it was twice a year or more but everyone could submit a framed painting and John Chirnside and John Howard would, between them, do the crit. It was mostly constructive criticism, but every now and then a 'hiccup' occurred, usually by John Howard. One Guild member brought a painting of his dog sat on a lovely green armchair. John Howard looked at it and said 'I can't understand what people are thinking of letting their dogs sit on chairs like that' to which the painter retorted 'it's my chair, my dog, and I'm not interested in your view on it.' He then promptly got up and walked out."

Barbara Brill, a journalist for the Stockport Advertiser, also attended a Criticism night around this time and wrote:

"Two meetings each summer are set aside for Art Guild members to bring their paintings for critical appraisal by two committee members [Chirnside and Howard]. The canvases are displayed alongside one side of the studio in St Peter's Square and are examined individually and comments and criticisms are given in front of an audience of members." She went on, "Landscapes and flower paintings predominated but there was a wide variety of individual styles and different methods of treatment. In the landscapes the faults were largely those of composition, perspective or choice of colour. The critics suggested how the faults could be remedied by the adding of a figure to give life to an empty street. In every case, they gave encouragement to the artists according to their experience, commenting on careful painting and on originality and boldness in tackling something different."

June Bevan (b. 1927)

June Bevan is another long-standing Guild member who also joined in the late sixties. She started drawing seriously from a young age and by the time she was sixteen had left school and was employed drawing engines for the Austin Motor Company during the Second World War. Three years later she changed jobs and became a tracer in the drawing office at Birmingham Town Hall, drawing out the city's new ring road. She spent her spare time drawing, painting and attending classes in the evenings.

Fig 81: June Bevan in 2018, with a self-portrait she painted in 1994.

Fig 82: A painting of Stockport College by June Bevan (1995).

She recalls when she started attending Stockport Art Guild sessions with great fondness:

"When I joined it was very highly respected and very difficult to get in. I didn't get in the first time I tried, but on the second attempt I was accepted to Full Membership and, joy of joys, I was thrilled. It was terribly important to me because I took painting very seriously. Joining the Guild back then was really something to aim for – it was very formal in those days."

By the eighties, Bevan was spending more time on her practice and regularly going on residential painting courses across the UK and abroad, including to John Blockley's studio in the Cotswolds; Greece, with renowned painter Paul Millichip, and to Southern India with watercolourist Lucy Willis.

In the mid-1990s, she enrolled onto the Foundation Course at Stockport College of Art and then went on to take a degree in Fine Arts with Liverpool John Moores University, graduating with a BA (Hons) in 2000. She found it hugely inspiring being alongside other like-minded artists:

"I think drawing is one of the most important things in life - drawing what you see and being observant. I would sometimes sit and sketch in a café or restaurant, usually wearing sunglasses because people do catch on and notice if you keep looking at them.

I've always used a sketchbook from the time when I first started painting. I'm all for getting the darks and like to use an 8 or 9b. Light is the most important thing to me in my work. I think a lot of people don't realize the depth of tone all around us really, especially when it's sunny."

Bevan has been exhibiting her work for over forty years and has had six solo exhibitions.

Fig 83: June Bevan's sketchbook (2003).

Stockport Air Disaster

At 10.09 am on Sunday 4th June 1967 one of the darkest events in Stockport's history occurred when a plane full of holidaymakers crashed in Hopes Carr, a street just 400 metres away from the Guild's studio in Peter's Square. The British Midland aircraft was on its way back to Manchester Airport from Majorca when it ran out of fuel due to a technical error in the fuel system. After avoiding a gasometer and a block of flats, it skimmed the roofs of some nearby houses before hitting the ground. Seventy-two passengers and crew aboard died in the accident but, miraculously, no one on the ground was injured. It currently stands as the fourth worst disaster in British aviation history.

Fig 84: The crash site of the 1967 Stockport Air Disaster.

The Studio

At the AGM at Peter's Square studio on 4th March 1968, twenty-one years after SAG had moved there, one of the members, Mr Chaloner, stood up and told the room that he had heard that plans had been drawn up for the redevelopment of St Peter's Square. His fear was that the Guild may lose their Studio and that they should start looking for new premises as soon as possible. John Chirnside, who was less panicked, calmly reassured the membership that he expected the Guild would be safe for the next few years and suggested members leave matters alone for the time being.

John Chirnside proved to be right. One year later, the Guild were still using the Studio and talk of moving wasn't even discussed. What was top of the agenda at that year's 50th AGM were the plans being made for a special celebration dinner and exhibition later in the year to mark their Golden Jubilee. President Chirnside declared:

> *"This year we reach our half-century of exhibitions. We want to make it something special. Lord Bowden of Chesterfield will open it, he is a brilliant chap. He disclaims any great knowledge of art but he has wide interests."*

Fig 85: The War Memorial Art Gallery in 1969, around the time of Stockport Art Guild's Golden Jubilee Exhibition.

The Guild's Golden Jubilee

The Golden Jubilee Exhibition was a spectacular show with many of the key Guild members putting in exemplar pieces. Lord Bowden opened the show on the 1st November 1969 to a packed room at the War Memorial Gallery. In his opening address he posed the question:

"What is it that after more than half a century makes such a group keep things going. The title? Who thought of calling the group a Guild? I think this has a lot to do with it. Like the Medieval Guilds which were formed to maintain standards of craft we are interested in making a good job. 'Technique' is considered to be almost a dirty word by some people, but we are interested in technique. Not just technique, but we stick to a sound job."

John Howard was chosen to write a piece about the history of Stockport Art Guild for the Golden Jubilee Exhibition catalogue:

"Affectionately known amongst many of the members as 'SAG'; but certainly not on any account of any wilting characteristics in the Guild which, on the contrary, happily has maintained upwards of 200 members over recent years.

The Annual Exhibition has long been considered the peak event of the Guild's programme year. To have reached the fiftieth is a splendid achievement and surely allows a backward look towards earlier days.

It must be rare when starting off an organization of our kind, for those responsible to imagine that historical details might be of any interest to those who follow on. It is more likely that immediate problems could seem sufficient burden. Such appears to have been probable with the Guild, so that available historical items are mainly attributable to individual memory rather than official record.

Stories of the early days suggest that a handful of painters, craftworkers and supporters used to meet informally in the residences of those who were prepared to be hosts, in order to discuss and practice their varied interests. In time, a constitution was formed and meetings became more formal and ambitious. Before the Guild acquired its own rented studio premises in St Peter's Square, members were permitted the weekly use of a studio, for a painting session at Stockport Art School. While this was a most valuable facility for the membership at that time, the occupation of the studio premises for the Guild's sole use heralded an important step forward.

Since that time the membership total doubled and a full programme of events ensued, including several regular meetings each week, for painting and drawing. Handicraft activities diminished, however, because of an inability to provide facilities at the new studio, together with a marked increase of interest in painting and drawing.

Much more could be written about Stockport Art Guild of likely interest, but what is necessary, is gratefully to acknowledge the foresight of those who established the movement years ago, and the many since, who have not only kept the Guild in being but have seen to it that progress has been maintained in a highly successful way. It would be invidious to mention names, both for the past and in regard to recent times, but none is forgotten for their varied and valuable contributions, in so many ways."

A new member of the Guild who exhibited two pieces in the Golden Jubilee exhibition called 'Unit Structure' and 'Dervish – Grey and Red' was Harry Turner (1920-2009).

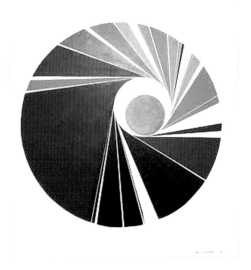

Fig 86: 'Blue Dervish', acrylic on hardboard, by Harry Turner (1968).

Harry Turner

Turner's artistic talent became apparent whilst still at school. By his late 20s he was working as the Advertising Manager at Redfern's Rubber Works in Hyde, which prompted his move from Manchester to Romiley in 1954. It was around this time that he joined the Beeches Art Group in Romiley.

During the 1960s his love of abstract art led to him to begin experimenting with business charts, from his job in the Advertising and Promotion Department at The Manchester Guardian, which he turned into paintings. He also became interested in the graphics of perceptual anomalies (optical illusions), influenced by the work of Josef Albers.

From an interview in 1984 Turner recalls:

"I painted some designs based on optical illusions in the 1960s—ideas largely borrowed from Josef Albers. I knew of Escher's work at the time, and had read Arnheim, Gombrich and Gregory on art and illusions. My preoccupation with visual ambiguities was sharpened in 1973 by an exhibition held at the London Institute of Contemporary Arts called 'Illusion in Nature and Art.'

I found the work of the Russian Futurists and Constructivists, of the British Vorticists - Wyndham Lewis, Edward Wadsworth, CWR Nevinson - to be of particular interest, although strangely neglected by contemporary art historians. For a while I painted geometric abstracts, mainly acrylics on canvas, with subjects that derived from mathematical concepts — dynamic symmetry and the geometries of form and growth, initially, then investigating 'dragon' and 'pathological' curves."

Harry Turner was a member of, and exhibited with, Stockport Open throughout the sixties and seventies. He was selected for the prestigious painting prize 'John Moores 8' in 1972 (the year that Euan Uglow won and Sean Sculley received a commendation), and was elected to membership of the Society of Modern Painters in 1976.

Fig 87: Harry Turner at home (circa 1970s).

1970s

New Decade, New Studio

Fig 88: LS Lowry discussing exhibited works (circa 1973).

At the beginning of the seventies it was the turn of Mr LJ Bowker, a landscape painter from a small village near Wem in Shropshire, to take over the Guild's Presidency. In his opening address at the AGM he remarked that:

> *"Our Jubilee Exhibition was one of our best. It compared very well indeed with other societies. We can be justifiably proud. Lord Bowden proved to be a satisfactory opener. He not only opened the exhibition, he also opened his cheque book."*

On a more cautionary note, John Chirnside said that:

> *"...although we had good attendances at our exhibition, sales should be better. It is up to every member to get wealthy acquaintances and friends to the exhibition."*

New Studio

On 17th March 1972, the landlord's solicitors wrote to the Guild giving notice on the studio at St Peter's Square. The owners of the building were going to demolish it and redevelop the land. It was exactly four years since Mr Chaloner had signalled that the Art Guild's days at the Studio at St Peter's Square were numbered.

The search began immediately for alternative premises. After a few months it became apparent that it was going to be very difficult to find anywhere as good as the current studio.

At the beginning of the decade, Stockport Metropolitan Borough Council (SMBC) introduced a scheme whereby all their Primary and Secondary Schools could be hired out to local groups in the evenings for a nominal charge. John Howard thought that this could potentially be a good option for the Guild in the short-term. So, in July 1972, he wrote to Mr Davey, the Director of Education at SMBC, requesting use of Pendlebury Hall School in Heaton Norris (formally the Stockport Secondary Technical School for Boys).

CLOSED ON SATURDAYS

BRIAN TAYLOR & CO.

SOLICITORS
COMMISSIONERS FOR OATHS

BRIAN TAYLOR

TEL 061-480 { 0277/8/9
              { 5798

92/96, WELLINGTON ROAD SOUTH,

STOCKPORT, SK1 3TJ

CHESHIRE.

OUR REF. BT/5738/SD.

YOUR REF.

17th March, 1972.

Messrs. A.H. Blackman, J. D. Howard & W. J. Colclough,
Stockport Art Guild,
4 St. Peter's Square,
STOCKPORT.

Dear Sirs,

Re: Studio or room on 2nd Floor of 4 St. Peter's Square,
Stockport.

We act for Birmingham Estates Limited of Desmicon House, Newby Road, Hazel Grove, the owners of the above property and we are instructed to give you Notice terminating your tenancy on the 29th September, 1972.

You will see that our Clients would oppose an application to the Court for a new tenancy, because on the termination of the current tenancy our Clients intend to demolish the premises, prior to a comprehensive redevelopment.

We understand that our Clients' agents have already indicated these proposals to you and we should be glad if you would acknowledge receipt of this letter.

Yours faithfully,

Fig 89: The tenancy termination letter for the Guild's St Peter's Square Studio (March 1972).

S. A. G. (printed letter paper).

as from:

9. Park Avenue,
Cheadle Hulme,
Cheadle, Cheshire,
SK8 6EU.

15th July, 1972.

C.G. Davey, Esq., M.A., B.Sc.,
Stockport Director Of Education.

Dear Mr. Davey,

Request for use of a studio

The property in which the Guild has rented a studio room for 25 years is to be demolished for 'development'. Accordingly we are to vacate the premises by the 29th September.

Much of the Guild's success can be attributed to the possession of the room for members' sole use, for lectures, demonstrations and so on, as well as for drawing and painting sessions. In order to continue the latter activity we wondered whether you would kindly consider allowing the Guild the use of a studio at the Pendlebury Hall school premises, until such time as we are able to obtain a place of our own once again. (We are not finding the search an easy task, but we shall continue trying, of course).

We have planned to hold the final painting meeting in our room on the 18th August, and it would be excellent for us if we could please start at Pendlebury Hall on the following Friday, the 25th August from 7.0pm. until 9.0pm., and weekly thence-forward.

The Guild has been meeting for these painting sessions on three evenings each week, for many years, with a total weekly attendance of 35 - 40 members. We think, however, that it might be best to plan in respect of one evening, weekly, with a maximum attendance of perhaps twenty members for the time-being.

Would you be so kind as to let me have your views and an outline of the conditions required of our members in the welcome event of the Guild being allowed the use of a studio at the school?

Yours sincerely,

JOHN D. HOWARD,
vice - Chairman.

NB. As no reply had been said to the above, the director's office was approached, by 'phone, on the 13th Sept. + an appointment made to call at the Town Hall on the 18th Sept. The correspondence dated the 13th + 14th Sept. ensured. Mr. John Hall joined me at the Town Hall, and in a visit to the Hollywood School. J.H.

Fig 90: The letter requesting use of Pendlebury Hall School (dated 15th July 1972).

Following a meeting between John Howard, John Hall and the Education Committee, it was agreed, that instead of hiring Pendlebury Hall School, the Guild would hire Hollywood Park School in Edgeley.

The Guild moved out of their St Peter's Square studio on the 29th September 1972 and transferred to their new space, an upstairs classroom at Hollywood Park Primary School. They agreed to rent it for the use of 'painting classes, lectures and demonstrations' every Monday and Thursday evening at a cost of £5 per session.

Members quickly settled into a routine of Monday night portrait and a Thursday night life drawing sessions. The autumn and winter programmes of demonstrations and lectures continued, as did the summer outdoor sketching trips.

Fig 91: The rental agreement to use Hollywood Park School (dated 14th September 1972).

Twinning with Beziers

In 1972, thanks to Gillian Lund who was the International Liaison Officer at Stockport Council, the Guild began a new and lasting relationship with the Societe des Beaux Arts in Stockport's twin town of Beziers, in France.

SAG members began sending paintings annually to the huge international Salon Exhibition held each spring in the Palais des Congres in Beziers. In 1978, the Guild enjoyed major success when it won the Salon's award for the finest group of paintings submitted by an art society.

In return, the Societe des Beaux Arts exhibited in the Guild's Annual Exhibition at the War Memorial Gallery. The exhange scheme continued until 1999.

Fig 92: XX11me Salon de la Société des Beaux-Arts Catalogue.

Les Artistes de la "STOCKPORT ART GUILD"
(Angleterre)
Cité Jumelle de Béziers

INVITÉS d'HONNEUR

W. E. BARTRAM
1	Brancaster	Aquarelle

J. M. BEVAN
2	Parkland	Huile

J. CHIRNSIDE
3	Sima (Persian girl)	Pastel

A. CHURCHOUSE
4	August 1977	Aquarelle

M. K. DEAN
5	On Finlow Hill	Huile

W. L. FRANCIS
6	Delamare Forest	Huile

D. M. HALL
7	Riverside trees	Aquarelle

J. HALL
8	New Galloway Read	Huile

M. HAYWOOD
9	Estellenches	Aquarelle

J. D. HOWARD
10	River Bollin	Huile

D. JENNINGS
11	English Landscape	Huile

J. LEES
12	Kettlewell	Aquarelle

A. J. MAYHEW
13	Langsdale	Aquarelle

C. V. FRYKE
14	Silence	Huile

G. ROBERTS
15	Blue Mantle	Huile

R. SWIFT
16	Fabruary	Huile

F. TIDESWEL
17	Summer Flowers	Huile

E. WILLCOCK
18	Poppies	Huile

M. WILLIAMS
19	Part of Old Knutsford	Aquarelle

H. YATES
20	White Sands Bay	Aquarelle

Les Artistes du Cercle des Beaux Arts d'HEILBRONN
(Allemagne Fédérale)
Cité Jumelle de Béziers

INVITES D'HONNEUR

CHRISTMAS Alex
21	Le Baptême de Jésus	Gravure peinte
22	Trois gardiens	id
23	Outrage à la civilisation	Sérigraphie

BERTSCH Joachim
24	Industrie florissante (77)	Technique mixte
25	Le programmeur	id
26	Nuages	id

HAUSLER Otto
27	L'église de Horkheim	Gravure
28	Méditation	id
29	Le vieillard alerte	id
30	Portrait dn professeur W. JENS	id

ERGUL Erlem
31	Forêt en Automne	Huile
32	Les arbres	id
33	Nostalgie de la natura	id
34	Villageoise	id

CORNELIUS Reiner
35	L'Allgau après la pluie	Huile
36	Le jardin de la Poste au lac Amer	id
37	Le lac de Wurs près de Hanovre	id

MAISAK Walter
38	Cheval dans la forêt	Peiture au couteau
39	Ferme dans la forêt bavaroise I	id
40	Ferme dans la forêt bavaroisn II	id
41	Cavalier sur la plage	id

MAIER Walter
45	Nature morte aux citrons	Huile
46	Nature morte	id
47	Nature à la guitare	id

HOPFENSITZ K.
48	Message clandestin	Huile
49	Gaspard HAUSER	id

SPITZER Werner
50	Paysage de rêve I	Peinture sur bois
51	Paysage de rêve II	id
52	Paysage de rêve III	id

CIETER Salomon Hans
53	La danseuse	Aquarelle

KOSTER Annedore
54	Improvisation grecque : Mistra	Dessin à la plume
55	Improvisation grecque	id
56	Improvisation grecque : Nani	id

Fig 93: XX11me Salon de la Société des Beaux-Arts Catalogue.

Fig 94: Salon de la Société des Beaux-Arts in Beziers.

Jack Lees

Jack Lees was a member of the famous Stockport felt hatting family, T & W Lees. The family firm was established in the town in 1870 by his grandfather, Thomas Lees, who had also been Mayor of Stockport. As well as working in the family business Jack Lees was a Major in the Territorial Army and travelled the world with them. During his spare time he was an enthusiastic amateur artist and was very keen on drawing and painting with watercolours.

In 1966, the company merged with four other local hatmakers to form Associated British Hat Manufacturers Limited. This allowed him to dedicate more time to his passion, art, and in 1971 his friend John Hall persuaded him to join Stockport Art Guild.

Jack Lees had been a member of the Guild for three years when he was elected onto their Council in 1974. His initial role was to deal specifically with exhibition publicity such as organising the catalogue, posters and liaising with the local newspapers. The effect of his involvement was immediately seen

Fig 95: 'Car Park' by Hal Yates (1973).

as the exhibition that year broke all previous sales records. The Stockport Advertiser reported, "With two weeks to go before the exhibition closes, over 50 works – paintings and sculpture – have been sold to the value of over £1,000."

Jack Lees introduced the practice of the Guild Council having their meetings at the Red Bull pub on Middle Hillgate (rather than at Hollywood Park School), a tradition that continued for almost a quarter of a century. Some of his paintings still hang in the bar there.

He became SAG's Honarary Treasurer in 1977, a role he continued until his death in 1988.

In 1975, Guild Member Christine Garner was asked to model at one of the regular Monday night studio sessions at Hollywood Park. She recalls:

"I'll never forget John Chirnside asking me to sit as the model hadn't turned up. 'Come on Chris jump up on the platform.' He did a fantastic portrait of me and I could see he was chuffed with what he had done. Anyway, several weeks later he asked me whether I would mind my portrait being put in his forthcoming exhibition, 'Ooh I said I'd be honoured.' It was a gorgeous painting, not because it was of me but because it was alive.

Mum and I got to the exhibition and it'd only been open half an hour, and I went up to him and said 'Mr Chirnside can I buy that picture of me?' Well his face dropped and he said 'Chris I've sold it. I didn't think you were interested' and then he said 'Look I'll come to the studio one night and I'll do some pictures of you' – which he did."

Fig 96: Pastel from life by Bill Bartram (circa 1974).

Fig 97: 'Christine Garner' by John Chirnside (1975).

Fig 98: 'June Bevan' by John Chirnside (1972).

Christine and LS Lowry

LS Lowry was known to give encouragement to young amateur artists and this was demonstrated in 1973 when he visited Stockport Art Guild's Annual Exhibition at the War Memorial Gallery. Christine Garner recalls an encounter with him:

"I remember the first pastel I ever did – it got onto the Annual Exhibition – I think it was 1973. I went to the exhibition the following weekend after it had opened to have a look round while it was quiet. Anyway, Cliff, the caretaker at Stockport Gallery, said, 'LS Lowry is in, would you like me to introduce you?'

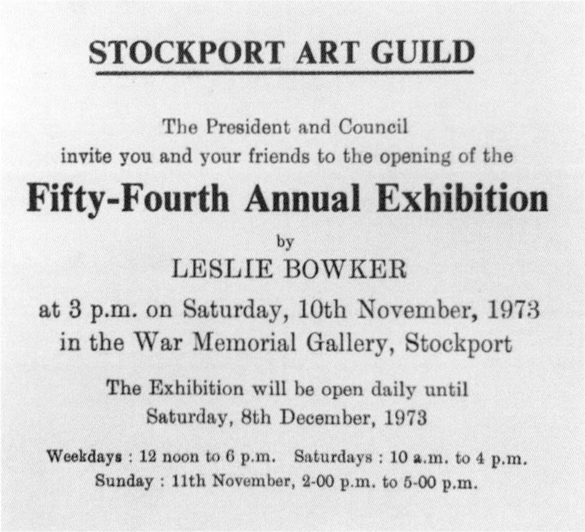

STOCKPORT ART GUILD

The President and Council invite you and your friends to the opening of the

Fifty-Fourth Annual Exhibition

by

LESLIE BOWKER

at 3 p.m. on Saturday, 10th November, 1973 in the War Memorial Gallery, Stockport

The Exhibition will be open daily until Saturday, 8th December, 1973

Weekdays : 12 noon to 6 p.m.   Saturdays : 10 a.m. to 4 p.m.
Sunday : 11th November, 2-00 p.m. to 5-00 p.m.

Fig 99: An invitation to Stockport Art Guild's Annual Exhibition in 1973, the year LS Lowry visited.

So, he took me and I shook hands with Mr Lowry. He kept going in his pocket for his pen, it never crossed my mind to get his autograph – I was just enjoying talking to him as it was a real deal to me. We got chatting and he said 'Have you got a painting in here?' So I told him I'd got a pastel and he said, 'Would you like me to give it a criticism? Tell me where it is and give me 20 minutes and then come and find me.' Twenty minutes later I went downstairs and he was still stood in front of it. He said to me, 'Did you say that was your first painting? Never stop painting.' I still didn't get his autograph, but this chance meeting with LS Lowry is mine alone, worth far more to me than an autograph. I have kept that first painting

I think he was lonely and he said to me, 'Everybody's making money out of my work but me'. Then he said, 'Do you live far from here? I could just go a cuppa' but I had no money on me and my car was off the road having a clutch done – how could I get him home? A chance in a million...missed."

Fig 100: A Pastel painting by Christine Garner, as seen by LS Lowry (1973).

LS Lowry and Stockport

Lowry had had a lifelong association with the town, from being an exhibition judge with the Stockport Art Guild when he was in his early forties to producing paintings of the town in his late eighties. He especially seemed to like visiting the town's architecture, with its tightly packed terraced houses and monolithic railway viaduct, which he included in many of his urban landscapes.

Rather than being confined to commercially acceptable and successful subjects, Lowry felt he was able to express himself more freely, like other part-time artists who painted purely for pleasure. His status as an amateur artist meant that he would come into contact with an art society like Stockport Art Guild, where people were happy to paint for passion and not for profit.

In the early 1930s there was a group exhibition at the Stockport War Memorial Gallery that included a painting by Lowry called 'Crowther Street, Stockport' showing a steep and curved Crowther Street with its banked terraces winding into the distance. Stockport War Memorial Gallery's Education Committee bought this painting at the time for just £30. Another painting in the same exhibition "Old Swanage, Dorset" by James Chettle was also purchased at the same time by same committee for £40. Interestingly, Chettle was still the 'art expert' on the committee by then.

Fig 88: LS Lowry discussing exhibited works (circa 1973).

Fig 101: LS Lowry on Wellington Steps in Stockport (1962).

The John Hall Years

By the mid-seventies it was John Hall's turn to become President and Chairman of the Guild. His friend Jack Lees joined him as Honorary Treasurer on the Council.

Another new member, Alf Churchouse, joined at the same time and he recalls:

> "*Jack Lees was a likable fella. He was a dominant character though – he'd been a colonel in the Cheshire Regiment. We always met in the pub because he used to go in there at lunchtime. He would sit there in the committee meetings and argue his head off until he got his own way.*
>
> *I remember one night in the pub, we were discussing the annual show and he said anybody who paid their subs should be entitled to have at least one picture of their choice in the show and we would hang it. I thought that was a good idea, if you'd paid your subs you were in. So we passed the resolution and that's what we did.*"

Alf Churchouse

Alf Churchouse was an amateur artist who worked as a civil servant in the centre of Manchester. In the mid 60s he decided to take his art more seriously and enrolled onto an evening class at the Manchester School of Art.

After he'd been there a while he was called before a committee, which he described as 'three worthies who were all experts in painting.' They wanted to point out to him that the colour of the sea in some seascapes that he'd recently painted wasn't the same colour that they saw. Churchouse replied quite nonchalantly saying that was quite possible because he was 60% colourblind. The three representational artists didn't know how to deal with this revelation, so they recommended Churchouse joined a new class that MSoA were starting up on Friday nights called 'experimental painters.' MAFA member Terry McGlynn ran the group.

McGlynn was widely regarded as one of the last of the 'Manchester Bohemian' artists. His work was influenced by Abstract Expressionism and continually challenged accepted values. His teaching style focused on the creative rather than the representational aspects of painting. This suited Churchouse and the other artists in the class perfectly and he remembers:

"There was another artist there who worked at a printers. Anyway, he had a roller you used for putting the ink on the printing press and what he used to do was put his paint directly on the roller and you used to get all sorts of effects. We were quite fascinated by it.

I used to find it particularly difficult with a blank sheet of paper making a mark and starting. And then when you'd made a mark, when do you stop? That was the next thing that intrigued me."

From this moment he became an abstract painter and never returned to representational art. In the 70s, the City Art Gallery in Manchester announced they were putting on an exhibition of artwork done by the city's civil servants. Churchouse saw this as a great opportunity to show off what he'd been producing and so put work in the show. He remembers visiting the exhibition:

"I was walking around there one lunchtime before I went to my office. Another civil servant was there stood in front of my picture; he was about four grades up from me. Anyway, he said he knew a man who was in the Guild and asked me why I didn't join. So I did.

John Chirnside and them knew about doing a portrait or a landscape, but had no idea about critiquing abstract work. Nevertheless, after a while, more abstract painters turned up so I wasn't on my own in the end."

Alf Churchouse joined the Guild Council in 1979, was promoted to Vice-Chairman the following year, and was elected Chairman in 1986. He served as President from 1998-2000.

Fig 102: Alf Churchouse in 2017, with one of his abstract paintings.

A Strong Exhibition

The Guild's Annual Exhibition of 1976 took over the whole of the War Memorial Gallery and consisted of over 270 works. Wilfred Colclough, who by this time was an Honorary Life Member and had been exhibiting in the Guild's Annual Exhibitons for over forty years, showed a series of watercolours of Snowdonia. Other artists on show that year included: June Bevan, Christine Garner, Harry Turner, Alf Churchouse and Jack Lees.

A month later, in January 1977, the Stockport Advertiser reported the theft of a painting by Jack Lees from the entrance hall of the Stockport Central Library. It was a painting in a scheme called 'Picture of the Month' that Stockport Art Guild and the Stockport Central Library were running at the time. Lees told the newspaper that the theft was particularly awkward, as he had only loaned the picture. It had been sold some time ago, and he had only asked for it back on loan from the owners, as it was a painting of the library and he thought the subject was 'particularly suitable for the occasion.'

Fig 103: The poster for Stockport Art Guild's 57th Annual Exhibition in 1976.

Diamonds are Forever
(Committees are not)

By the time of Stockport Art Guild's 60th Anniversary in 1979, it had grown into one of the largest art societies in the North West and built up an enviable reputation.

To mark their Diamond Jubilee, the Guild commissioned John Chirnside to paint a self-portrait that was then presented to Harry Dodd, the Mayor of Stockport. After it had been on display in a special Annual Exhibition at the War Memorial Gallery, it was to be hung in the Town Hall. John Hall, who was still President that year, wrote to all past members asking them to submit a painting to the exhibition which they had painted when they were members.
The Stockport Advertiser, writing about the Guild's landmark anniversary, said:

> *"The old saying 'Diamonds are forever' will be bandied around the studio of Stockport Art Guild this coming autumn, for they are looking forward to celebrating their Diamond Jubilee and laying plans for the future."*

Fig 104: Self-portrait by John Chirnside (1979).

Fig 105: John Hall presents a self-portrait by John Chirnside to the Mayor in 1979.

One thing that wasn't forever was the status quo on the Guild Council. At the end of 1979, Bill Bartram and the three Johns all announced their retirements. Alf Churchouse vividly recalls the occasion:

"When they retired from the Council, almost en bloc, we thought what are we gonna do, because nobody wanted to be on the committee. They ran the Guild the way they wanted.

So at their last AGM, Chirnside had the idea to put everyone's name in a hat and whoever got pulled out would have to go on the committee. I remember we all sat there in the room at Hollywood Park and it was plainly obvious that some of these old ladies that were there were never going to join. So Bill Bartram stood up and said we would re-run the election and I remember seeing him pushing these tickets around and deliberately picking out the names he wanted – it was the election according to Bill. Anyway, that was when I found myself on the committee."

Amidst all this change, a new face emerged onto the scene by the name of John Blakeley. Stockport Art Guild welcomed him with open arms for he was a rare breed amongst their members… he was a sculptor.

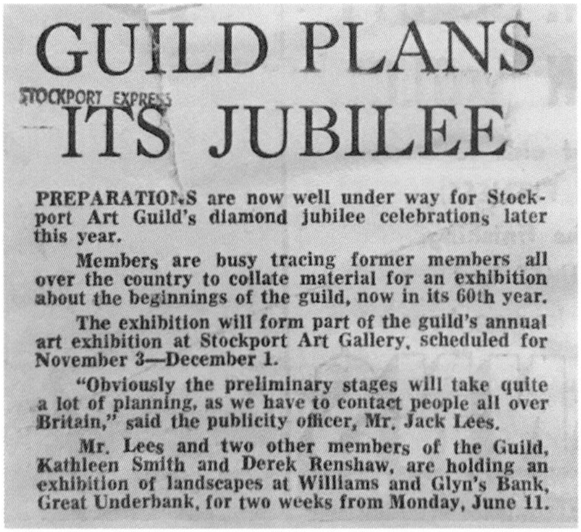

GUILD PLANS ITS JUBILEE

STOCKPORT EXPRESS

PREPARATIONS are now well under way for Stockport Art Guild's diamond jubilee celebrations later this year.

Members are busy tracing former members all over the country to collate material for an exhibition about the beginnings of the guild, now in its 60th year.

The exhibition will form part of the guild's annual art exhibition at Stockport Art Gallery, scheduled for November 3—December 1.

"Obviously the preliminary stages will take quite a lot of planning, as we have to contact people all over Britain," said the publicity officer, Mr. Jack Lees.

Mr. Lees and two other members of the Guild, Kathleen Smith and Derek Renshaw, are holding an exhibition of landscapes at Williams and Glyn's Bank, Great Underbank, for two weeks from Monday, June 11.

Fig 106: Stockport Art Guild's Diamond Jubilee celebrations, as reported in 1979.

Fig 107: Stockport Art Guild members 'en plein air' in the late 1970s.

Artistic merit recognised

Stockport Art Guild members are pictured discussing a picture of by-gone Stockport painted by Mr Robert Williams (right) of Hazel Grove

TS 3816

FIVE new full members, elected from the associates' class on merit, were adopted by Stockport Art Guild following the associates' exhibition at their studio at Hollywood Park School last week.

They are Mr Roger Williamson, Mrs Phyllis Boon, the Rev Sister C. Kelly, Mr G. W. Douglass and Mr Tom Spencer.

The criticism was given by Mr Wilfred Colclough, one time head of the art department of Stockport Grammar School and now life member of the guild, and the vice-chairman Mr Harry Allcock.

Refreshments were provided by Mrs K. Smith.

Fig 108: A newspaper article in 1979 about newly elected 'Full' Members.

Recognition all Round

Fig 109: (detail) 'Jimmy and Toots' by Mike Heath (2000).

John Blakeley was unanimously elected to replace John Hall as the Guild's President at their 60th Annual General Meeting in March 1980. He had only been a member of SAG for one year.

John Blakeley

John Blakeley is an internationally acclaimed sculptor. He was born in Salford in 1928 but his family had moved to Stockport by the time he was five. He initially studied painting and drawing at Stockport College before heading to Italy to study sculpture at the Carlos Nicoli Sculpture Studio.

Blakeley's transformative break came in 1967 when he was commissioned to create a bust of Joseph Smith, the ninteenth century founder of the Mormon Church. John travelled 8,000 miles to Salt Lake City, to take precise measurements from Smith's death mask, and to personally oversee the quarrying of the half-ton block of marble that he used to create the bust. He was reported as saying:

"When you're working with Carrara marble you can only do it once. It's not like a painting you can change and change, once you do something to that marble, it's done forever."

Blakeley remained SAG President until 1983 when he left the Guild.

John Hall painted a portrait of John Blakeley that was shown in the 1980 Annual Exhibition at the War Memorial Gallery. Blakeley exhibited a sterling silver sculpture entitled 'Midnight'; a bronze called 'No Quarter' and a 14ct gold sculpture called 'Day Old', for sale for £11,000.

Standing firm

In the spring of 1981, it emerged that SAG's annual November time slot for their exhibition had been reserved by another exhibition and, as a result, it looked like the Guild were unlikely to have a show at the War Memorial Gallery that year. Blakeley immediately arranged a meeting at the Town Hall on the 16th April 1981 with Mr Simpson, the Assistant Director of Recreation and Culture at Stockport Metropolitan Borough Council.

Two weeks later Mr Simpson wrote to John Blakeley apologising for the disagreement and confirmed that the Guild's 62nd Annual Exhibition was back on track for the 7th – 28th November 1981. He said:

"I am pleased to be able to tell you that we have managed to re-arrange the dates to accommodate your requirements. I should add that this has been achieved by postponing one ehibition and by curtailing another.

I am sorry that we reached a position of disagreement between the Guild and ourselves. As I said at the meeting, I appreciate the contribution that the Guild makes to the arts in Stockport. We wish to see the Guild continue to flourish and we are very pleased to house the Annual Exhibition in the Art Gallery. I hope that we can continue to co-operate as we have done in the past.

In order to ensure that the pictures look at their best may I remind you that there should be a maximum of 230 pictures in your exhibition. All our other conditions are the same as for last year.

I hope that this clears up all our outstanding problems and I look forward to another high quality exhibition in November."

The exhibition that year had over 230 artworks on show and was a fantastic example of the diversity of the membership at that time. Works included a number of pieces by Alf Churchouse, June Bevan, Bill Bartram and Jack Lees. John Blakeley had two bronze sculptures in the exhibition entitled 'Yearling' and 'Louise.'

One of Stockport Art Guild's long-standing and highly regarded members, Mike Heath, joined the group in the early eighties.

Mike Heath

When Mike Heath was young he attended evening classes at Stockport College where he began drawing in pencil and started to use oil paints. Mike fondly remembers walking home from there regularly feeling elated after a productive lesson.

He joined Stockport Art Guild as an Associate Member in 1982 after another Guild member, Mike Pendleton, phoned him and suggested he started coming along to the Thursday evening life drawing sessions at Hollywood Park School.

Heath's early drawings were all done in 2b pencil until, one night at the Guild, he observed a couple of artists using pastels and was inspired to try them out. He immediately liked the medium and, within no time, was producing some successful artwork.

One particular drawing that he did at a Monday evening session, around 2000, was a sketch of a gentleman holding his dog that he called 'Jimmy and Toots.' It only took about an hour and a half to do but is one of his most popular pieces – it was also his first time entry into the Stockport Open.

It wasn't until 2001, when he was asked to join the Guild Council, that he applied and was accepted as a Full Member. Once on the committee, he took on the responsibility for booking and setting the portrait night models, a role he continues to perform every Monday.

In 2018, after 17 years, Mike Heath resigned from the Guild Council. Although very busy with voluntary work, he says his Monday and Thursday evenings at Stockport Art Guild are still the highlight of his week:

"It's a matter of encouragement and being there. Sometimes, you arrive and

don't feel up to it, and then you start to get into it and drawing becomes instinctive. When things become instinctive, that's when you get the best results. It might be the last two minutes of a session when you forget yourself and the drawing just flows."

Fig 109: 'Jimmy and Toots' by Mike Heath (2000).

The painting exchange programme with Stockport's twin town of Beziers continued throughout the eighties, with Guild members sending paintings every year to the huge Salon Exhibition there. In 1983, June Bevan was one of the artists that took part and she recalls:

> "All the Guild members were asked if we'd like to put a painting in to send to Bezier – and we packed them all up and somebody sent them all off. The painting I submitted that year was called 'The Chimneys of Stockport' and it was awarded a commendation in their show."

Fig 110: In 1983, June Bevan's painting 'The Chimneys of Stockport' was awarded the Diplome d'Honneur in Bezier.

One of the artists from the Societe des Beaux Arts that exhibited with the Guild in 1983 was Sylvie Laforet. Her observational paintings captured the fringe elements of society, such as hippies and the homeless, with a sense of humour and satire. She sent three pieces to Stockport that year entitled 'Jeunes Hippies', 'Jeune Hippie' and 'Le Poete.'

Stockport Art Guild's Annual Exhibition that year also included a special display of work curated by exhibition sponsor, Dennis Robinson of Robinsons Brewery. He asked all the SAG members if they would like to paint a horse and dray at their Brewery. A number of artists did, including Bill Bartram, John Hall and Tom Spencer. At the exhibition, Dennis Robinson chose Bill Bartram's painting as his favourite; it was subsequently purchased and now hangs in Robinson's Head Office.

By the mid-1980s the Guild was still operating with three main classes of membership: Full Membership, which cost £5 a year; Associate Membership at £4 and Junior Membership for £2.50. Associate and Junior Members were

Fig 111: 'Jeunes Hippies' by Sylvie Laforet (1983).

given the chance to move up to Full Membership on Election Day by submitting between three and six original works to be judged by the Council. SAG's rules at the time did state, however, that 'in special cases entry may be direct into Full Membership at the discretion of the Guild Council.' There were also 'Distinguished Life Memberships' and 'Honorary Memberships', by invitiation only.

By 1985, the Hollywood Park School building had stopped being used as a teaching establishment and was now vacant most of the time (apart from the local societies like the Guild that rented it out from Stockport Metropolitan Borough Council). As a result of the space no longer being manned, SAG members were no longer able to safely leave their equipment or unfinished paintings in the studio. The building was becoming unloved and the lockable cupboards that the Guild used to store their materials had also been vandalised and broken open a number of times.

The Mayor of Stockport, Councillor Eddie Lowe, receives one of eight paintings, drawings and sculptures presented to him by members of Stockport Art Guild last Friday. The works will now hang in the mayor's parlour for visitors to enjoy. The Guild has a studio in Hollywood Centre, Hardman Street. Pictured are: Harry Hitchcock, president; Jack Lees, treasurer; Alf Churchhouse, vice-chairman; David Beattie, secretary; John Docker, Ralf Badger, Agnes Barlow, June Bevan and Phillis Boon.

Fig 112: A cutting from the Stockport Express Advertiser (14th March 1985).

So, in June that year, the Guild Council took the decision to start to build up enough capital to either buy outright or rent exclusively some premises of their own. A special fundraising sub-committee was formed to lead this project. One of the things they introduced to build up enough money to get their own studio was a members' lottery. Shares cost just 50p a month to join the Guild's '250 Club' and from the money collected half was paid out in prize money (1st prize £15) and the rest was invested, with the aim of buying a studio.

Also in 1985, the Stockport Express Advertiser began an annual award scheme with Stockport Art Guild that ran in conjunction with their Annual Exhibition. The newspaper's editor awarded a prize and a trophy for the painting, or sculpture, which he found to be the most pleasing. In the first year, editor Barry Bettany chose a pastel painting by Kathleen Smith as the inaugural winner of this trophy. The scheme ran for ten years and other winners included Marjorie Dean, Agnes Barlow and Mike Pendleton.

Fig 113: The Stockport Express Advertiser Annual Award Trophy.

Jack Lees Certificate of Merit

The Guild's 1988 Annual Exhibition saw the introduction of another award, the 'Jack Lees Certificate of Merit.' This was conceived to commemorate Lees' death that year and to acknowledge the great contribution that he had made to the Guild. Certificates of Merit would be presented every year for pieces that the Guild Council felt were of outstanding quality. This award continued for the next twenty-five years and was highly regarded amongst members.

Joan Bradley was one of the Guild members that won numerous Jack Lees Certificates of Merit over the years.

Joan Bradley

Bradley grew up in Beswick, East Manchester, and is one of ten children.

Towards the end of the 1970s she was accepted into Manchester Polytechnic to study Fine Art. Barry White, the renowned abstract artist, was the senior lecturer who saw her work and was immediately impressed. Barry believed in experimentation in art and instilled that in his students. He once said:

"Making a painting is a process of discovery, an uncharted creative journey in which I have no preconceived idea of the final image. I hope that my paintings evolve as I evolve. Every work has to be a new experience with an element of risk-taking. You've got to be able to surprise yourself."

After graduating from Manchester Polytechnic, Bradley moved to Hong Kong and continued her practice. Whilst there, she exhibited in Queens Road Gallery and in the Wanchai Arts Centre. On returning to Manchester, three years later, she became a part-time art lecturer for Manchester Adult Education Services.

She joined Stockport Art Guild in 1989, after hearing about the group from her friend Patricia Niemira, who was a member at the time. Bradley recalls:

"Two months after joining I was a Full Member and a couple of months after that I was Secretary. It was the Annual General Meeting and Carole Mountain, the Secretary at the meeting, asked if anyone could type and I put my hand up, and she said I would be the Secretary."

Bradley was on the Guild's annual Adjudicating and Hanging Committee for many years and enjoyed getting members' work on show each year and being part of an artmaking community. She readily admits, however, to not missing the stress of the official side of organising an exhibition.

Joan remained SAG's Honorary Secretary until she became their Chairman in 1998, a role she kept for seven years. Such was her contribution that by the end of her Chairmanship she had earned the nickname 'Joan of Art.'

In 2000, she was elected a Fellow of the Royal Society of Arts.

Today, Joan continues to paint every day and works from her studio in Stockport's Vernon Mill. She passionately believes in continually evolving her paintings to ensure that they stay fresh – an ethos that her old tutor, Barry White, would wholly concur with.

As the 1980s drew to a close, the Guild still hadn't found any new premises and was still using the Hollywood Park Building. All this, however, was about to change: they had received a letter informing them that Stockport Council were planning to demolish the building - they needed to find new premises as soon as possible....

Fig 114: Joan Bradley with one of her paintings (2018).

The Gallery that became Home

Fig 115: 'Shops and Bollards (Stockport)' (detail) by John Dronsfield (2008).

By the start of the nineties, Bert Mayhew was comfortably settled into his new role as President of the Art Guild. He had assumed the role, at short notice, in July 1989, after the sudden death of Harry Hitchcock. His immediate mission was to find and help the Guild settle into a new home. The fundraising sub-committee was doing well with the lottery, the '250 Club'.

However, there was always the perennial problem of finding suitable premises for the Guild to use as a Studio. The solution came after a conversation with John Sculley, the curator at the War Memorial Gallery. He offered the use of the Gallery on Monday and Thursday evenings to hold the Guild's sessions. Very quickly, agreement had been reached with the Metropolitan Borough Council and the Guild moved into their new home.

Alf Churchouse, the Chairman at the time, recalls:

> "It was a much better proposition (than Hollywood Park School), it was clean and tidy and spacious and it was being used for art. The council staff were very helpful too."

Members quickly settled back into their routine, with the additional benefit that they were now producing their art in the venue in which it would be exhibited. In the Guild's April 1991 Newsletter, Honorary Secretary, Joan Bradley, wrote: 'I think everyone will agree that we made the right choice in moving to the gallery...'

1991 ended with an excellent Annual Exhibition that included works by Joan Bradley, Patricia Niemira, Agnes Barlow and Ken Slack. One of the Jack Lees Certificates of Merit that year went to a new Associate Member, John Dronsfield, who was exhibiting with the Guild for the first time.

Following the Annual Exhibition, the Guild's newsletter expressed disappointment that sales were down on the previous year. Their Treasurer, Edna Harrison, reported that 27 paintings had been sold with a combined value of £1,530 compared with 34 paintings the previous year worth £2,256. The UK recession had tightened its grip and was resulting in high interest rates and falling house prices.

Inflation was in double figures, which meant lower consumer spending – most people simply weren't in a position to buy luxury items such as paintings.

John Dronsfield

John Dronsfield had had a successful career as a lecturer in design and graphics at Manchester Polytechnic. He took early retirement in 1990 and was then able to spend more time developing his own work.

To aid this progression, he joined Stockport Art Guild around 1991. Despite being awarded the Jack Lees Certificate of Merit at the Annual Exhibition, he was rejected for Full Membership that year. The Guild however recognized his talents on his second attempt and he was duly promoted.

John Dronsfield quickly became involved in the Guild's activities and was soon made a member of the Council. He quickly became a judge on SAG's Adjudicating and Hanging Committee and was regularly involved in their 'Criticism Evenings', which he preferred to call 'appraisal of work' evenings. He also gave talks to the membership on various aspects of his work. He liked to be thought of as a 'father figure' for the Guild.

He was elected President of the Guild in 2000, a role that he retained, apart from one year, until 2013. He lived in New Zealand from 2004-6 with his wife, Carole.

Dronsfield is an accomplished painter whose subject matter centres around dwellings (which reflect the soul), water (making up much of the human body), ships (the transportation aspect) and natural forms and their struggle for survival. When asked about his practice, he says:

"Each picture starts with a story or an idea, to communicate on a number of different levels to reach a wider audience, so it is chameleonic in nature. Watercolour allows me to float and be instant and ethereal; acrylic I tend to use for larger works; gouache and inks are colour weaponry...I use these to zing

Fig 116: 'The House Without a Boat' by John Dronsfield.

with and exploit the use of colour as a powerful agent, to excite, motivate and infiltrate the mind, to fill it with fun. It is emotional magic, a world full of wonderment."

Grumbles at the Gallery

At the Annual General Meeting in 1992, now held at the War Memorial Building, Bert Mayhew's Annual President's Address began with a special thanks to Bill Bartram, who had recently had a stroke and was no longer able to serve on the Adjudicating and Hanging Committee. Bartram passed away in 1995.

Bert Mayhew's speech also touched on the success of the new studio nights at the gallery, which were getting record attendances. There were some issues with the sessions, however, and a lively debate followed. Mayhew pointed out that he felt time was being wasted with the models walking about chatting for a long time and that he thought these should be kept short as the model was being paid for their two hours' work. Other members expressed that they wanted the studio nights to be quiet and have a 'business-like atmosphere with no break and a continuous drawing experience.'

Chairman Alf Churchouse was a fully committed abstract artist by this time and never drew or painted the models. Despite this, he recalls having to turn up every week at the life drawing sessions:

> *"I couldn't get anyone to pay the model, not a single one of them would give her the money we had to pay her. I had to go. I was there under duress. So I used to find a table in the other room and whilst the others were painting the model - I would just paint my abstracts."*

In 1993, the Guild filled the whole of the War Memorial Gallery with over two hundred and eighty works for their 74th Annual Exhibition. It was an impressive display that had been chosen by the esteemed members of the Adjudicating and Hanging Committee: Alf Churchouse, Agnes Barlow, Joan Bradley and MK Dean. The Jack Lees Certificates of Merit that year went to June Bevan, Joan Bradley, Barbara Dale and GT Hooper.

The 74th Annual Exhibition also saw three new Associate Members exhibit for the first time. John Stephenson had a painting called 'L'Enfant Garde' accepted into the show, and husband and wife artist duo, Angus and Faith Yeaman, showed 'Etherow Trees' and 'September in Sancerre' respectively. The second half of the decade also saw Annette Bonelle, Marjorie Dean and Pauline Wiltshire join Stockport Art Guild.

In July 1996, the Guild Council raised the model fees to £4.50 for the portrait and £7.50 an hour for the life model. This was in line with what other art societies paid and Ken Slack confirmed that the models were happy with that. As a result of this increase, the studio attendence fees were raised by £1.50 per session.

Bert Mayhew announced that 1997 would be his final year as President and that the Guild would need to start the search for his successor. At the Council meetings throughout the rest of the year there were regular discussions about who might replace him. At the May monthly meeting Alf Churchouse pointed out that:

> "The position is one of a figurehead and that the person chosen should have something to do with Stockport and possibly art. The person needs to act as a referee, someone aloof and not involved in the day to day running of the Guild."

At the Annual General Meeting on the 23rd March 1998, the Guild's next President was finally unveiled. Proposed by Joan Bradley and seconded by Faith Yeaman, Alf Churchouse resigned as Chairman and was formally elected President. Bradley replaced Churchouse as Chairman.

At the AGM in March the following year, as another decade came to an end, Alf Churchouse said in his opening address that it was pretty remarkable to belong to an organisation that has survived for so many years. Little did he know that within the next ten years the people responsible for the gallery that they called home would endanger the Guild's very survival!

The
2000s
The Decade of Change

Fig 117: (detail) 'The Birling Gap' by Ron Coleman (2018).

The new millennium saw a host of new faces join Stockport Art Guild including Christopher Rose-Innes, Carole Dronsfield, Karen Wise, Stephen Johnson and Ron Coleman. Another significant name that came on board at this time was the self-taught artist Angela Herd Hall.

Angela Herd Hall

Before becoming a full-time artist, Angela Herd Hall was a draughtsman and network planner for a telecommunications company. Her work is mainly figurative and she cites Egon Schiele, Peter Coker and Tim Benson as her inspirations.

She became an Associate Member in 2000 but it took two years before she was elected to Full Membership of the Guild. She recalls how the society felt back then:

"I started with life sessions on the Thursdays. It was elitist back then, you had to take your drawings and be accepted as a Full Member and all that malarkey. People who were there when I started going were Mike Pendleton, Mike Heath, John and Barbara Wood. Ken Slack was the guy who ran it – he booked the models.

In 2004 I joined the Council as the Thursday night model setter – taking over from Ken Slack."

She tends to work in oils, acrylics and graphite from her garden studio. Portraiture and life drawing are a key focus in her practice and she finds the figure endlessly fascinating

Fig 118: 'Aunty Winnie' by Angela Herd Hall (2013).

"I am lucky enough to be able to work from life and costume models every week, and most of my work is alla prima. I try and draw every day. It's the basis of my work and I am, perhaps, old-fashioned in my belief of the importance of it."

In 2018, she was accepted into the Manchester Academy of Fine Arts. The Annual General Meeting in March 2000 saw John Dronsfield replace Alf Churchouse as Guild President. Joan Smith and Faith Yeaman also took over as Honorary Secretary and Honorary Treasurer respectively.

Fig 119: Angela Herd Hall in her studio (2018).

Fig 120: 'The Skipper' by Mike Pendleton (2001).

Mike Heath, John Stephenson, June Bevan and Philip Harding were awarded the Jack Lees Certificates of Merit at the 81st Annual Exhibition in November 2000. New Associate Members, David Gledhill and Angela Herd Hall, also exhibited that year. Herd Hall, recalls a funny story from around this time:

"I remember one night at the life drawing - one of the members collapsed on the floor. So we had to call the ambulance because they were out cold. But it was life night, so when the paramedic came and saw a nude life model sitting there he was highly embarrassed and blushed to a deep shade of red - you

could see that it was totally out of his conception. Anyway, it was so funny, and so British, because the rest of the group just carried on drawing as the casualty was taken away. They happily recovered in a couple of days."

Christopher Rose-Innes

(Christopher Rose-Innes was a Professor of Physical and Electrical Engineering at UMIST from 1964 until his early retirement in 1989. In his spare time he was a keen amateur sculptor and treated his art seriously.

At the age of 63, with more time on his hands, he did a Fine Art degree specialising in sculpture at Manchester Polytechnic and graduated with 2.1 honours.

Rose-Innes joined Stockport Art Guild as an Associate Member in 2001 and was elected to Full Membership in 2003. He remembers the occasion clearly:

"In those days there were two classes of membership, Associate Membership and Full. And you had to have three pieces of work accepted into the show to be promoted up to Full Membership – and your subscription went up too!

The sessions in those days were in the upper gallery - I remember the first time I went, there was a portrait class already in session. And so I sat down and drew, and strangely enough I've never done a better drawing - and so they said oooh you must be quite good."

His sculptures are mainly made in wood, stone or clay and range from abstract to portraiture and from tabletop to public sculpture. He likes to experiment rather than develop a distinctive style and says:

"A lot of my sculptures are based on the human form, usually in a rather stylized manner. I think going to life drawing helps my understanding of how the body is articulated. I don't want to just make a realistic figure like a Victorian marble sculpture; on the other hand I want it to be recognisable. And

so I try to strike a balance between stylisation and realism.

For example, one of my sculptures 'Home Assembly Man' (circa 2000) is a three-quarter life-size of a man sitting down. It was 2D made into 3D with three sheets at right angles."

Christopher Rose-Innes is a member of the Royal Society of Sculptors and the President of the Stockport Art Guild (at the time of writing).

Fig 121: Christopher Rose-Innes at work in his studio.

Fig 122: 'Home Assembly Man', made of Redwood Pine, by Christopher Rose-Innes (2000).

The Guild again had use of the whole of the Gallery for the 83rd Annual Exhibition in November and December 2002 and over three hundred pieces of artwork filled the building. The artists who exhibited that year included Stephen Player, Pauline Wiltshire and Elizabeth Brickhill; and the Jack Lees Certificates of Merit went to Inez Jackson, Roy McClachlan, Mike Pendleton and Margaret Royle.

Christopher Rose-Innes was still an Associate Member in 2002 and exhibited three sculptures, 'The Temptation of Adam', 'Trinity' and '3-Strand Plait.' He recalls:

"What was quite amusing was to stand by my work at the Annual Exhibition to hear what people have to say. They don't know you're the artist, and so I'd often hear the inevitable 'Ooh I like that…but I'd have nowhere to put it.' That's the trouble with being a sculptor."

At the Guild's AGM on the 16th February 2003, everyone agreed that their 83rd Annual Exhibition, which had finished a few weeks earlier, had been a great success with regards to the quantity, variety and quality of work that was on display. There was a sense of disappointment however that only 15 paintings had been sold, compared to 22 the previous year.

Hopes turned to the 2003 Annual Exhibition, which was formally opened on Saturday 21st November by Kenneth Holt, the Mayor of Stockport. There were 298 pieces on show in the Art Gallery, including arwork by Maggie Preston, Sarah Morley and John and Carol Dronsfield.

Carole Dronsfield

Carole Dronsfield first started glass engraving in the early 1970s. A decade later she founded the Peaks and Plains Branch of the Guild of Glass Engravers, and in 1987 she was elected as a Fellow of the Royal Society of Arts.

Her expertise with cut and stained glass and the playful way that she uses light and shade to bring engravings to life earned her a great reputation.

Nevertheless, she recalls the first time she applied for Full Membership of the Guild:

"I went through the assessment process twice before I was accepted as a Full Member. For my initial assessment, the glasses I submitted were small delicate pieces on clear glass...no colour involved. I suspect that there was no one on the assessment panel who knew what to make of my work.

On the second occasion I submitted much bigger work which featured engraving and stained glass work.... with lots of colour. That seemed to help and I was given full membership."

Unfortunately, due to visual migraines, she was unable to continue working on glass and so she ventured into working in pastel. She soon fell in love with what she described as 'a freer, larger and altogether more relaxing medium' and particularly enjoyed the intensity of colour and the joy of gently merging tones together.

After living in New Zealand from 2004-6, John and Carole Dronsfield returned to Stockport and quickly re-established themselves as key players within the Guild. She joined the SAG Council in 2006 and a few years later was elected Vice-Chairman. They both announced their retirement from the Guild Council in July 2013.

Fig 123: Glass engraving 'Underbank Hall Stockport' by Carole Dronsfield (circa 1985).

Fig 124: John and Carole Dronsfield (2018).

Despite the optimism that preceded the 84th Annual Exhibition in 2003, the consensus, at the Guild Council meeting after the show, was that it wasn't as good as in previous years. The conclusion that they drew was that Associate Members were now gaining Full membership more easily than before and that this was leading to an increase in the amount of naïve work ending up on the gallery walls.

It was also felt that the Exhibition Selection Committee were now tending to be less rigorous in their judging of Associate Members work. So, at the 2004 Annual General Meeting, members were kindly reminded that it was the quality of work that counts in a SAG exhibition and members were requested to only put forward paintings and sculptures that they thought represented their best work. There was also a debate at that year's AGM around the Jack Lees Certificates going to the same people each year and so it was decided that whomever was awarded a Merit would then be excluded from winning again for four years.

Fig 125: 'Tupping Out' by John Wood (2004).

Ron Coleman

Before becoming a full-time artist, Ron Coleman spent his life travelling the globe installing, analyzing and repairing, what were then, state-of-the-art complex computer systems. Since taking a three-year Open College of the Arts course in the 1990s, he has specialised in abstract expressionist painting. Coleman joined the Guild in 2004 and recalls the time he first heard about the society:

"I was at the Stockport Open and I met Annette (Bonnelle). She talked about my work and said to me, why don't you join Stockport Art Guild? So I started coming to the Monday night portrait and also the life class. I remember feeling that everyone was there for a constructive two hours and that they wanted to take their practice seriously, which I really appreciated.

It took a little while to get to know people, everyone used to keep to themselves. There were people there who were just starting to draw and also very accomplished artists like Mike Heath and Angela Herd Hall."

Many artists and movements have influenced his practice, from the St. Ives abstract artists and the American Expressionists to the Scottish Colourists. He takes an 'alla prima' approach with his abstract work and likes to use colour, form and texture to create his compositions. His paintings are generally completed in one or two sessions:

Fig 126: Ron Coleman in his studio.

"I want to create work that appeals to people's visual senses, balancing form and colour in a way that attracts the viewer's attention, and perhaps holds their gaze long enough to allow them to engage with the painted surface.

My small abstract expressionist paintings, for example, are intended to be uplifting and contemplative in nature. These paintings are balanced by the handling of colour relationships, use of texture and vibrant brushwork. Although there are intended and accidental juxtapositions of colour, the resulting painting has a harmony that comes from the careful and thoughtful arrangement of form and colour.

Creating a good abstract painting is hard work and my initial ideas can often result in failures. Success sometimes comes unexpectedly but most usually as the result of a 'moment of inspiration' when everything comes together."

Ron Coleman became an elected member of the Manchester Academy of Fine Arts in 2016.

Fig 117: 'The Birling Gap' by Ron Coleman (2018).

Doreen Leach was elected President at the Guild's Annual General Meeting in 2005; Joan Bradley became Chairman and Annette Bonelle was made Honorary Secretary. The Council members that year included Ken Slack, Mike Heath, Joan Smith, Pauline Wiltshire, Alan Wynne, John Clements and Angela Herd Hall.

John Dronsfield was living in New Zealand by this time but kept an eye on proceedings from afar. Despite not being the Guild's President or a Council member that year, he clearly still felt close ties to the society and sent a speech to be read out at the AGM. It included these words of wisdom:

"There is still an existent snobbery about art materials, with oils as the prima donna in painting, bronze in casting and jade or greenstone in the carved world. Forget these petty distinctions and use what is the best for you. Firstly, the best for your character, your nature and sensitivities, then for your pocket and your workspace. Some mediocre painters have become top class potters/sculptors once they gave up trying to be what they and others thought they ought to be."

The Rise of the Machines

A motion was proposed at the 2005 AGM as to whether the membership should accept photographs and computer-enhanced images into their Annual Exhibition. A lively debate followed with some members very much against it, whilst others felt that the Guild needed to adopt the modern media. The vote was called and the motion was rejected 2:1. Adobe may have just acquired FreeHand, the illustration software, from Altsys but computer imagery was not about to be accepted by the Guild.

By the mid-noughties, one billion people worldwide were using the Internet. The fears of Y2K, the Millennium bug, had come and gone uneventfully and the vast majority of businesses, organisations and even art societies had committed to having their own website.

Neil Robinson, Guild member and soon to be Web Master on the Council, launched the first incarnation of the Stockport Art Guild website later that year. He recalls:

"The question of getting a website came up in conversation at one of the Guild Council meetings. I mentioned that I'd recently completed a City & Guilds course in website design and that I could create a web presence for us. Everyone loved the idea, so I came up with designs and mock-ups, and the website was launched at end of 2005.

On the menu page, I designed what was known as an 'image map' which basically illustrated the inside of Stockport Art Gallery with links to various pages like a news page and a gallery of artwork represented by icons such as Rodin's The Thinker."

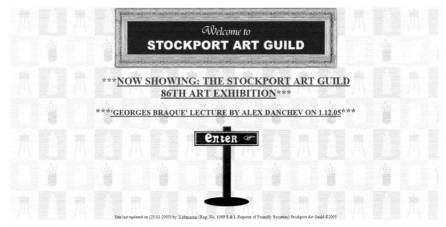

Fig 127: Image of the Stockport Art Guild's first website (2005).

Fig 128: Image of the Stockport Art Guild's first website (2005).

Robinson's design also included a section on the website where every Guild member could display their own artwork. There was also a news area with information about forthcoming art demonstrations; details about the society's Annual Exhibition and a virtual photo wall. To add some fun to the website, he also incorporated a drawing app called 'Draw Easy,' which allowed users to create coloured patterns on the screen.

Fig 129: Ron Coleman, winner of a Jack Lees Prize in 2005, with Deputy Mayor Burns and Doreen Leach.

Change was at the top of the agenda at the Council meeting in March 2006. There was a lengthy discussion about how Stockport Art Guild could be 'more dynamic.' It was felt that other local art societies were overtaking the Guild and that:

> "...we were being overlooked and regarded as rather amateurish and so were not being invited to get involved in other exhibitions or art ventures on the internet."

The 87th Annual Exhibition was held, as usual, at the War Memorial Gallery. The opening, on the 25th November 2006, was very well attended with around 300 invited guests. Members in the show that year included Angela Herd Hall, Ron Coleman, Neil Robinson, Pauline Wiltshire, Karen Wise and Christopher Rose-Innes.

2007 – Lest We Forget

At the start of 2007 the Guild had 199 members comprising: 86 Full, 95 Associate and 18 Honorary Members.

The AGM on the 26th March 2007 began by welcoming John Dronsfield back to the UK and announcing that he was to be reinstated as Guild President. Joan Bradley remained Chairman and Christopher Mollen became the Vice-Chairman. It was also announced at the meeting that Ron MacLachlan, a wonderful artist and distinguished Life Member, had sadly died, aged 99 years. It was unanimously agreed that, as a mark of respect, six of his pictures would be hung at the Annual Exhibition later that year.

At the AGM, the Guild discussed a proposal from Peter Fox, the curator of Saddleworth Art Gallery, to hold an exhibition of work by Stockport Art Guild members in the summer of 2008. This offer was unanimously accepeted and it was agreed that the Council would get in touch with the gallery in Uppermill to discuss details.

In the spring of 2007, a new Arts and Cultural Events Manager at Stockport Metropolitan Borough Council wrote to the Guild announcing that the SMBC Arts Team, along with the staff at the War Memorial Gallery, were undertaking a major review of all the current and future activities at the gallery, including the Guild's Annual Exhibition.

Sensing the potential gravity of the situation for the Guild, Joan Bradley, Janet Rigby and the rest of the membership pulled together. On 4th October 2007 a special meeting was held between the SMBC Arts Team and seventy-five Guild members - it was a show of unity of which Walter Foster, the society's inaugural President, would have been proud.

Sadly, the outcome did not go in favour of the Guild. A major international exhibition called 'Fragile State: Art From Kosova' had already been confirmed for the time that the SAG Annual Exhibition was due to take place. The Guild show had to be cancelled for that year – the only year since its formation that they didn't have an annual display.

Although this was clearly a huge disappointment for Stockport Art Guild, the War Memorial Gallery was the perfect venue for 'Fragile State: Art From Kosova.' This internationally significant show, which ran from 20th October 2007 until 5th January 2008, featured the work of nine Kosovar artists who had documented life inside Kosovo during the 1990s civil war. Ismet Jonuzi, one of the Kosovan artists, describes his sculptures:

Fig 130: 'The Accursed Mountains Cycle' by Agim Salihu.

> *"The concept behind my work is about peace. From weapons I explain my story of the reality of war in Kosova. These are weapons that people fought with. Somebody died from this. Barrels of guns, machine-guns, Kalashnikovs and knives that are made to take lives and destroy them. I have used them. I build sculptures out of them. Through shape, line and volume I have tried to express the drama that we have experienced as a community in this part of the Balkans. These weapons have been put beyond use in a way that gives them new life. The sculptures act as a reminder and warning of the destruction caused by conflict as well as providing a beacon of a new life and renewed hope. My work represents the wounded soul of my homeland."*

Bronwen Simpson, who was part of the team at Stockport War Memorial Art Gallery at the time, says:

> *"The permanence of this new-found use of weapons struck me immediately. It is impossible for these guns to ever be used to kill, maim or destroy again. What better way to openly demonstrate war is over."*

Agim Salihu, another of the artists in the show, explains:

> *"Process is very important – the physical act of inscribing into metal - of digging out - of creating the scar lines on the plate that then create the lines on the faces. They appear out of the darkness and act as a constant reminder of what has been before as well as highlighting how interpretation of history can change our perception of the past."*

This powerful exhibition was showing at the War Memorial Gallery during Remembrance Day in November 2007. The 1919 Education Committee, who set out the founding principles for the use of the War Memorial building, would have been pleased.

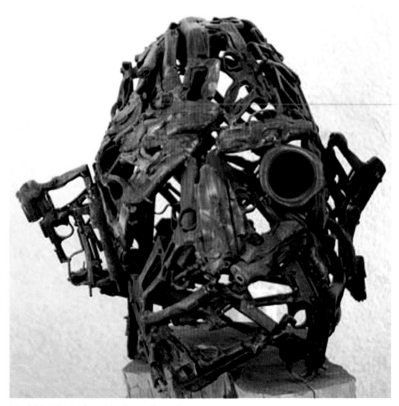

Fig 131: 'The Helmet' by Ismet Jonuzi.

Immediately after the special seeting between Stockport Art Guild and Stockport Metropolitan Borough Council (SMBC) on the 4th October 2007, the SAG members that were present stayed for an Extraordinary General Meeting to discuss the structure of the Guild membership going forward. A resolution was raised to determine if there should be a single membership on joining or whether the two levels, Associate and Full, should continue as it had done for 88 years.

After a heated debate, the motion was carried to abolish the status of Associate Member and so in future all new Guild members would automatically become Full Members the moment they paid their subscription. This was a significant moment for the society, as it had had an elected membership since its formation in 1919.

A new era had begun – the Guild's doors were now open to everybody.

Fig 132: The Stockport Art Guild 2008 Spring Exhibition Poster, designed by Neil Robinson

Fig 133: 'Pears' by Angela Herd Hall. Exhibited in SAG's 2008 Spring Exhibition at the Saddleworth Art Gallery.

One Year Out

2008 was a busy year for Stockport Art Guild.

The Saddleworth Art Gallery Spring Exhibition took place from from 21st March to 20th April 2008 with twenty-eight Guild members exhibiting sixty-four works. A couple of months later, on the 7th June 2008, the Guild's 88th Annual Exhibition (in their 89th year) opened at the War Memorial Art Gallery, albeit in a much reduced form. Around one hundred works were on display, approximately two-thirds down on the usual numbers.

Fig 134: An advert for Stockport Art Guild's 2008 Annual Exhibition.

Fig 135: The 88th Stockport Art Guild Exhibition Preview at the War Memorial Art Gallery (2008).

In 2009, John Dronsfield and Joan Bradley continued with their respective roles of President and Chairman, however Carole Dronsfield joined them at the top table this year, taking on the role of Vice-Chairman. The other Council members that year were: Christopher Rose-Innes, Ron Coleman, Diedre Montgomery, Stephen Johnson, Karen Wise, Michael Hartley-Rose, Angela Herd Hall, Peter Holt, Mike Heath and Neil Robinson.

The Annual General Meeting took place on the 7th March 2009 at the Millbrook Centre in Stockport, a meeting venue that the Guild had started to use since 2007. The President's address talked about some of the ongoing issues with the Gallery and he pointed out that other local art societies were looking to have their work exhibited at the gallery and were, in effect, in competition with the Guild. Dronsfield also spoke about another art society that had had problems in the past but had fought against the recession and had become successful again; something he said he hoped would happen to the Guild.

Annette Bonelle, in her capacity as Honarary Secretary, then stood up and spoke about membership levels, saying:

> *"In the previous 12 months we have lost 39 members and 22 of those had only been members for one year. It is a cause for concern that we lose so many members shortly after they have joined. I think we need to find some reasons for this and to try to address the issue."*

It was recorded in the 2009 minutes that the Guild Council felt membership levels had dropped by a quarter as a direct result of the cancellation of the 2007 Annual Exhibition and reduction of the gallery space in 2008, 'making it impossible to hang one piece of work for every member'.

On the 12th June 2009, Stockport Metropolitan Borough Council confirmed that the Guild's Annual Exhibition that year would be held from the 10th October to 14th November. Peter Ashworth, Head of Arts, Culture & Visitor Attactions, wrote to Chairman Joan Bradley saying:

> *"The Art Guild's Annual Exhibition at the Art Gallery will continue on the top floor of the Gallery and will take place for at least six weeks in the last quarter of each calendar year (October, November, December).*
>
> *We recognize that there is a real need to showcase local artists at the Art Gallery...and we look forward to sustaining the Council's long relationship with the Guild."*

Stockport Art Guild's 89th Exhibition opened at the War Memorial Gallery, as agreed, on Saturday 10th October. The adjudication panel that year was John Dronsfield, Christopher Rose-Innes and Alan Thompson, a non-Guild member. Thompson was a friend and ex-student of Guild legend, Harry Rutherford. During the late fifties he studied painting under Rutherford at the Regional College of Art in Manchester.

The Guild continued to have a reduced gallery space that year and so only 117 works were accepted into the show. Nevertheless, it was an impressive display and

'Quick poses' - Thursday studio '09 by Angela Herd Hall

89TH ART EXHIBITION
10th October - 14th November 2009

Venue: Stockport Art Gallery, Wellington Road South, Stockport, SK3 8AB.

A selection of drawings, paintings, printmaking, sculptures and mixed media by members of Stockport Art Guild.
www.stockportartguild.org.uk

Preview on Saturday 10th October 2009.
Time: 1 pm - 4 pm.
Light refreshments provided.

Opening Times:
Tuesday - Friday: 1 pm - 5 pm
Saturday: 10 am - 5 pm
Sunday: 11 am - 5 pm
Closed Mondays

Stockport Art Guild

Fig 136: The 89th Stockport Art Guild Exhibition Poster, featuring a life drawing by Angela Herd Hall.

members who exhibited artwork included: Stephen Johnson, who submitted three Venetian scenes; June Short who displayed three sculptures and Karl Elphick, who not only sold his painting 'Untitled', but also picked up a Jack Lees Certificates of Merit for it too.

Following the drop in membership, SAG embarked on a big publicity drive at the end of the decade. Flyers were produced describing the Guild as 'The largest art group in the region with studio evenings Monday and Thursday at the Stockport Art Gallery, demonstrations monthly and an annual exhibition.' Stockport Art Guild desperately needed to pick themselves up, dust themselves off and start all over again... their very existence depended on it.

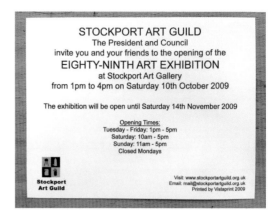

Fig 137: An invitation for Stockport Art Guild's 89th Annual Exhibition (2009).

Fig 138: Angela Herd Hall collecting her award at the 89th Stockport Art Guild Exhibition Preview (2009).

The
2010s
Fighting the Good Fight

Fig 139: (detail) Phil Hughes in his studio.

The Guild entered the decade with rekindled energy and drive. They wanted to learn from their recent experiences and put the last few difficult years behind them. One of the prevalent ideas was to allow more interesting and diverse work into the Guild's Annual Exhibtions. John Dronsfield in his President's address at the 2010 AGM said:

> "The Council has discussed at length the exhibition format and in the light of comments from the public and some from members of the Guild, these suggestions should not be seen as a change in policy, but rather a modification that should result in a more stimulating exhibition, that would sit more comfortably with the members' perception of what the Guild is about.
>
> We propose that more works per person could be submitted, thereby giving more choice. Provided that members submit two or more pieces, then one work will have guaranteed entry to the exhibition. This would mean that a piece of work that was perhaps not of great aesthetic value, or technical competence, could still find a place, and might well represent the unusual or alternative view that would lie outside even the wider accepted practise."

The foreword in the 90th Annual Exhibition Catalogue that year overtly described the show as 'an exhibition that will contain something for everyone' from a 'society whose membership embraces artists of all abilities.' They were clearly determined to be seen to have listened to everyone's comments. As a result, the exhibition had forty more pieces on display than the previous year and the diversity of work on show included: an aquatint etching by Irene Garner; a silk painting by Bill Hague; an embroidery by Judith Todd and a sculpture made of 'spring clips' by Christopher Rose-Innes.

Speaking about the exhibition, an executive member for Stockport Leisure at the time said:

> "Stockport Art Guild has played an important part in the local community for many years and its members have made significant contribution to Stockport Council's permanent collections."

SKarts

Despite the challenging economic climate at the end of 2010, a handful of enthuastic artists including Deirdre Montgomery, Ron Coleman, Sylvia Glover, Joan Bradley and Bridget (Midge) Mullally decided to start a voluntary group called SKarts.

Within six months they had relaunched the Stockport Open exhibition, describing it as a platform for artists in Stockport and the surrounding region to show, sell and be promoted. The 'Open Contemporary,' as it was called, had their first exhibition at the War Memorial Gallery from the 25th June to 24th August 2011.

Meanwhile, the Guild's 91st Annual Exhibition took place at the War Memorial Gallery from 29th October 2011 to 8th January 2012. One of the visitors who came to the exhibition was the artist Geoffrey Key. During his visit he raised the idea of a possible liaison between The Salford Art Group, that he was part of, and Stockport Art Guild. A month or so later, John Dronsfield and Geoffrey Key chatted about a number of potential collaborations, ranging from a combined get together between both groups to a web link on each group's website. Unfortunately, nothing came of these suggestions.

Recipients of the 2011 Jack Lees Certificates of Merit included Marlis Pantall, Sheila Vaughan, John Brindley and a member who had only joined the year before, Bert Yates.

Fig 140: Stockport Art Guild's Annual Exhibition in 2011.

Fig 141: Karen Wise next to her painting at the 91st Stockport Art Guild Annual Exhibition Preview.

Bert Yates

Herbert Yates (known as Bert) is a Manchester-based professional artist who joined the Guild in 2010. He recalls the reason he decided to give SAG a try:

"I needed a life class that had longer poses so that I could paint, as opposed to doing quick drawings. The two last sessions at each month were 2-hour sessions with a quarter of an hour break, which is plenty to do a small oil.

Drawing or painting from a nude is most important; it's like a training thing because the naked figure is so hard to do. It's something to measure yourself against and keep your drawing up to scratch. Whether it's landscapes, or still life or portraits or anything I think it starts there."

Yates lives in an inner city area of Manchester called Ancoats and paints the urban landscape around him. He says the nearest thing he has to the natural world are the wastegrounds full of tough wildflowers, unkillable weeds, discarded fridges and furniture. Nevertheless, he draws inspiration from these spaces and says that the very process of starting to draw or paint opens his eyes and imagination to the potential of wherever he happens to be.

For the past few years he has been developing his own tempera-style technique using acrylic. In his 2018 painting "Autumn Morning, Oldham Road" it can be seen how he builds up the form within the image using small, repeated vertical brushstrokes, which

Fig 142: Bert Yates with his painting "Autumn Morning, Oldham Road" (2018).

are very tightly packed. The majority of colours within this piece fall within the lighter end of the tonal spectrum, which gives it its deliberately high key look.

He was elected into Manchester Academy of Fine Arts in 2018 and joins a growing list of current Guild members who are part of MAFA.

Fig 143: A sketch by Bert Yates, done at a Stockport Art Guild life session.

Despite SAG's Annual Exhibition being back on the gallery's calendar and the Guild Council's unofficial policy of encouraging artistic diversity into their exhibition, many long-standing members had either still not renewed or were now just not as engaged with the show as they were in the past. In his 2012 President's address John Dronsfield clearly defined the dilemma:

"We have a serious deficiency in the number of members submitting work for the exhibition. Only about a third of the members put items in for selection. In the past, during the curatorship of John Sculley, we had sufficient quality

submissions to fill the Upper gallery and both the East and West galleries downstairs. Not only that, following adjudication, the upper landing would be quite full of non-selected works which shows that the adjudicators had plenty of work from which to choose a good exhibition.

Following the unprecedented cancellation of Stockport Guild's Annual Exhibition by John Sculley's replacement, the Guild Council has fought long and hard for its reinstatement. Eventually this was granted but we are now limited to the Upper Gallery. There have been extended negotiations to try to reclaim the East and West Galleries but to no avail.

Well, the news that I have for you is that, had we even had one of the downstairs galleries, we should not have been able to fill it, had we used all of the work submitted. At this rate of decline, after 91 years, this is an unusual scenario for a visually creative group. The Stockport Art Guild does not exist merely for its own cosy existence but to promote the visual arts in the town and encourage young artists, and children of all ages in our varying means of expressing our personal and developing self-expression.

The Guild Council has made several direct and indirect attempts to discover the reasons for this fall in submissions. I have drawn up a list of possibilities, which include: being too busy to submit; ill health; unable to afford the cost of materials and feeling that the work is not good enough...well...exhibiting is a good learning process, inability to cope with criticism or rejection...this is part of the activity and a normal part of life.

Only the members not submitting work can supply the reasons for non-participation. If you have a reason, please respond to the President or Members of the Council and communicate your feelings. If they can help, they will. The Council cannot respond to the members' needs and worries, if those points are not aired. This is an urgent matter."

Regardless of the issues with the Annual Exhibition, the weekly sessions felt like they had a newfound sense of energy. It had been five years since the Guild had abolished their Full and Associate Membership classes and as a result the group was now much more inclusive.

The Society's elitism of the past had been replaced with the feeling that everyone was welcome. They had started to see the arrival of some exciting new members that were using the Guild for a multitude of different reasons - Phil Hughes was one of them.

Phil Hughes

Phil Hughes is a figurative artist who works in oils and acrylic. He has a background as an architect in the UK and the Middle East and has been a visiting design tutor at the Universities of Cardiff and Liverpool.

The accuracy required in his profession contrasts with his artistic practice where, rather than planning his paintings in great detail, he prefers to get something down quickly and then work it, pushing the paint around until something clicks. He works in oils and acrylics and especially enjoys finding ways to use vibrant colours in his compositions. He gets inspiration from artists like Paul Ruiz and Mark Demsteader.

He joined the Guild in 2012 having heard positive things about it from other artists:

"The main attraction for me was the fact that the Guild provides regular portrait sessions: there are numerous life sessions around Manchester but not so many portrait groups and it's portraiture that mainly interests me.

Fig 139: Phil Hughes in his studio.

The fascination with capturing faces and figures for me is in the way that a tiny dab of pigment can completely change the expression or personality of the subject.

Even the simplest portrait is rich in meaning and can instantly convey impressions of age, intelligence, background, mood or taste. I try to capture some of that, but it's also good to have ambiguity and something unresolved."

He has exhibited his work at venues throughout the UK including Sale's Waterside Open, Chester's Grosvenor Museum Biennial and the ING Discerning Eye at the Mall Galleries.

Phil Hughes joined the Guild Council in 2016.

Fig 144: A sketch by Phil Hughes, done at a Stockport Art Guild portrait session (2015).

More Budget Cuts

Another new face that had arrived on the art scene in Stockport by 2012 was local businessman, Peter Holt. He had been made aware of both SKarts and SAG through an Art Therapy course that he had taken. With his vast management experience, Holt saw the challenges that both art groups faced and immediately offered to help.

SKarts had lost some of their founding committee. So, alongside two other new members, Olga Shulayeva and Ché Finch, Peter Holt joined the organizing team for SKarts' second Open Contemporary in May and June that year.

By the time of the Guild Council meeting of the 5th September 2012, news had started to spread that, due to more budget cuts, Stockport Borough Council were planning to close the Gallery during the week. The SAG Council agreed that contingency plans needed to be drawn up so a letter went out to all 122 members - it was time to unite for action once again.

Peter Holt and Ché Finch headed the revolution and came up with the idea for SKarts and Stockport Art Guild to start a joint petition, on both paper and on the digital platform Change.org. Two weeks later the campaign entitled 'Stop the Closure of Stockport Art Gallery and War Memorial during the Week' was up and running.

The response was incredible. Over the next few months, a series of meetings took place between John Dronsfield (SAG), Peter Holt, Ché Finch, Deirdre Montgomery (SKarts) and Peter Ashworth (SMBC), and over 1,000 supporters signed the petition - the momentum was building to get Stockport Metropolitan Borough Council to reconsider their plans.

The Guild's 92nd Annual Exhibition took place, as planned, from 3rd November 2012 to 13th January 2013. The winners of the Jack Lees Certificates of Merit that year were Angela Herd Hall, Bobbski Mather, Ché Finch and Michael Hartley-Rose.

President Dronsfield delivered another rousing speech at the Guild's AGM in 2013:

"Look around our town centre...there is an atmosphere of dereliction, of closed shops and failed precincts of neglect and decay; of poverty and hopelessness. Yet at the same time many cities are thriving through investment. This investment is creating a new look, with different values.

Change is now taking different forms and our close neighbour, Salford, is changing its character though becoming a media city, attracting interest and revenue worldwide. Liverpool has an ongoing programme of regeneration that is totally changing its character.

What can all this possibly mean to the Stockport Art Guild? It means that we have to respond to change in a more proactive way. The Guild Council

*has worked hard this year on proposals for maintaining our place within this
'Museum.' The result of considerable brainstorming by SKarts and the Art Guild
Council has been a realization of ideas that could transform our Art Guild
built on strong traditions into a vibrant, exciting and go-ahead motivator in the
visual arts.*

*We cannot avoid change, but if you are leading it, there is a better chance of
getting where you want to be. Thank you to all those who have been working
hard on behalf of the Guild."*

Peter Holt updated everyone about the proposed closure of the Gallery and the
news that Peter Ashworth had informed him that SKarts's Open Contemporary, the
Photographic Society show and Stockport Art Guild's Annual Exhibition would all go
ahead that year. He had also been told that the War Memorial Gallery was now under
the direction of the Conference Venue Management team and that the mounting and
dismounting of exhibitions would also have to be done by the societies themselves
and without help from gallery staff.

The Guild Council that year included John Dronsfield, Christopher Rose-Innes, Carole
Dronsfield, Angela Herd Hall, Annette Bonelle, David Holt, Stephen Johnson, Mike
Heath, Michael Hartley-Rose and Peter Holt. Anglea Herd Hall recalls:

"Peter Holt was a breath of fresh air for the Guild. He had a new take on everything
– he had lots of ideas to do different things at the exhibition such as the freestanding
boards and including a TV one year to show work. He also worked out a way to install
the exhibition, because we'd never had to do that before. How we hang now is thanks
to him."

John and Carole Dronsfield announced their resignations from the Guild Council in
July 2013, saying that they felt there needed to be 'an injection of fresh people with
new ideas to bring new impetus to the managing of the Guild affairs.' After some
discussion, John Dronsfield agreed to continue in post until the 2014 AGM, but
Angela Herd Hall took over the role of Vice-Chairman with immediate effect.

6 >> NEWS

500 more jobs axed and gallery opening slashed in town hall cuts

■ Council set for £24m budget cuts by 2014

■ Art collection to be closed on weekdays

JENNIFER WILLIAMS

A TOWN hall plans to close its art gallery during the week and shed 500 jobs in a bid to save £24m.

Stockport council is reviewing all its cultural attractions, and their opening hours, as part of a package of cuts over the next two years.

The plans include closing Stockport Art Gallery, on Wellington Road South, on weekdays.

Currently the gallery opens between 1pm-5pm, Tuesday to Friday, with longer hours on weekends.

The cuts are part of a package of measures aimed at dealing with an expected £24m cut to budgets by 2014.

Another 500 jobs are set to go – on top of the 430 already cut since April last year.

Council chiefs hope most will be lost through voluntary redundancy.

Other plans include slashing £1.3m from youth services – partly through axing vacant management posts – and focusing regeneration on the town centre and not outlying areas.

'This is clearly a really tough budget'

Planning fees would also be increased, in line with changing national guidelines, alongside a raft of back-office savings across all departments.

The move will be discussed by Stockport council's executive next week before being put out to consultation.

Martin Candler, the council's Liberal Democrat deputy leader and finance chief, said he hoped for an 'open and transparent' conversation on the issue with councillors and the public.

He said: "There are further savings to find to balance future years' budgets and this will require changes to how the council delivers services and an acceptance of more risk.

"I am confident, however, that the work of the last two years gives us a firm base to work from."

Conservative leader Syd Lloyd said: "This is clearly a really tough budget but we are going to have to make sure that the cuts minimise the impact on front line services."

Labour leader Andy Verdeille said bosses had not yet been clear enough about their plans.

He added: "Opposition councillors haven't been able to see any of the background papers setting the justification for each cut, something which must be put right urgently."

CUT Stockport council plans to close its art gallery on weekends, and lose 500 jobs as it bids to slash £24m from the budget

Fig 145: A Manchester Evening News article (September 2012).

Carrying On

It started to feel as though Stockport Memorial Art Gallery had had a stay of execution. They had received in excess of 80 applications to exhibit there and now had art exhibitions planned-in every month until March 2014. SKarts held their 3rd Open Contemporary there in July and August 2013. But sadly this was the last year it took place as SKarts stopped shortly after due to lack of volunteer support. Around this time, Peter Holt was interviewed saying:

> "Any community needs an artistic undercurrent to it. If you take away the culture, then what's left? It's a very dry society without culture in it."

The Guild's 93rd Annual Exhibition went ahead in November and Mike Pendleton, in recognition of his long-standing membership, had a special section dedicated to his work. The Jack Lees Certificates of Merit ended in 2013 and were replaced with seven Category Prizes instead for best Portrait, Landscape, Figurative, Still Life, 3D, Wildlife/Animal and Abstract.

Christopher Rose-Innes took over as President in 2014, a role that he continues to do to this day. The rest of the Council that year included Chairman Angela Herd Hall, Vice-Chairman Stephen Johnson, Hon Secretary Annette Bonelle and members Mike Heath, Peter Holt and Michael Hartley-Rose.

At the following AGM, on the 26th March 2015, Peter Holt gave an update on the situation with the gallery. He said it had been two difficult years for the War Memorial Building but he was happy to report that:

> "There has been a big turnaround and the gallery had gone from being the worst attended to being the best attended facility of its kind in Stockport. There has been a wide variety of exhibitions, which has created a new dynamism about the place."

At the end of the meeting the President presented Peter Holt with a framed certificate honouring him with Distinguished Life Membership of the Guild in appreciation of all his hard work and unrelenting optimism when the gallery faced closure.

Sadly, Peter Holt was never able to make the most of his Life Membership – he died of cancer in June 2017.

Angela Herd Hall pays tribute to his strength of character:

> *"Peter Holt was a man of integrity, a true one off. He put his heart and soul into keeping the gallery alive and keeping the Guild going."*

Mike Heath sums up the short but incredible impact he made:

> *"He was instrumental in getting the gallery back on track and put so much effort into keeping the gallery open by petitioning to not have it closed when the gallery was due to by shut by the council."*

Carole Dronsfield reiterates their sentiments:

> *"There was a seriously big doubt about the future of the Art Gallery and, consequently, the future of the Stockport Art Guild and its connections with the Art Gallery. Like the rest of the Guild, I give thanks for Peter Holt whose untiring work helped to resolve those difficulties."*

The Guild's 95th Annual Exhibition took place from Saturday 28th November 2015 until 6th January 2016. There were 123 pieces on display with a great variety of subject and media. Work included a series of etching aquatint prints by Neil Robinson and some 3D stoneware by Marguarita Bradshaw.

Phil Hughes stole the show that year, winning the Portrait Prize and Overall Best of Show for his painting 'Dream On' and also a brand new Award sponsored by Ed Perry of the Colourfield Gallery for his portrait entitled 'Cissie.'

By the end of 2015 the Guild had 80 paying members and 18 Life Members. Fifteen new members had joined within the past 12 months – one of them was the social realist painter, Peter Davis.

Peter Davis

Peter Davis is a prize-winning contemporary artist and an elected member of the Manchester Academy of Fine Arts.

Towards the end of the 1980s he attended Manchester Polytechnic, initially doing a one year Foundation Course before going on to study Design for Communication Media.

After graduating, he worked for the next twenty-five years as an advertising creative in London and Manchester. The marketing campaigns he produced became increasingly centred on people using personal devices as their primary touchpoint and this has undoubtedly influenced his work as an artist. Davis adds:

"Zeitgeist is my ongoing series of paintings that explore the subject of humanity and its relationship with personal technology. Seeing people glued to their devices is so commonplace now that I don't think we give it a second glance.

My aim is to capture the spirit of the age and create contemporary portraiture that tells stories about our society through a strong visual narrative. Being able to transform the often-overlooked elements of contemporary life is something I particularly enjoy about my practice."

In 2015, the same year that he joined Stockport Art Guild, he took the decision to pursue his artistic

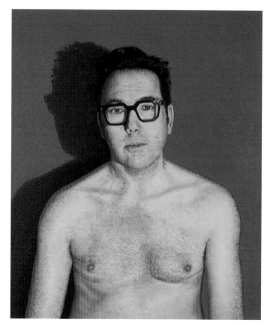

Fig 146: 'Face Furniture (self portrait)' by Peter Davis (2015).

career more seriously and since then has had a solo show at Warrington Museum & Art Gallery; been shortlisted for the international Aesthetica Art Prize 2018 and won several painting prizes throughout the UK.

Peter Davis joined the SAG Council in 2017. As a consequence of his enthusiastic work on preparations for the centenary celebrations in 2019 and the production of this book, he instigated and adopted the new role of Guild Archivist in 2018.

Fig 147: 'Cardboard Reality 1' by Peter Davis (2017).

At the AGM on the 21st March 2016, Christopher Rose-Innes continued with the rhetoric that John Dronsfield had set out during his presidency. Rather than a speech recalling highlights from the previous 12 months, he took a poll of all the members present that night, asking whether they wished the Guild to continue. There was a unanimous response that they did want the Guild to carry on. President Rose-Innes's response was emphatic:

> "If this is to happen then ALL members must play their part in running the Guild. Especially by joining the Guild Council. If we do not get volunteers, then the Guild will cease to function within the next few months."

The Guild's 96th Annual Exhibition took place from 3rd December 2016 until 7th January 2017. There were 152 pieces on show, which was an increase of twenty-nine on the previous year. The Adjudicating and Hanging Committee was made up of Marguarita Bradshaw, one of the winners from 2015; Christopher Rose-Innes, current President and non-Guild member Chris Clements, award-winnning figurative artist and founder of the Northern Realist School of Art.

Category Prizewinners that year included Bert Yates for his landscape 'Porthmadog Winter'; Stephen Johnson for his figurative painting 'Pat'; Ron Coleman for his still life 'Red Rose' and Inari Johnson for her animal picture 'Grateful Whippet.' Peter Davis picked up two awards that year: the Portrait Prize for 'Face Furniture (self-portrait)' and the Colourfield Gallery Award for his social realist painting, '8 tonight?'

The Stockport Metropolitan Borough Council (SMBC) re-established their Open Exhibition in the summer of 2016. There were almost two hundred and fifty entries and the show occupied all four galleries in the War Memorial Building. One of the guest judges that year was Bill Clark from the Clark Art gallery in Hale. He said:

> "The standard of work was really high this year and I was impressed by the diversity of the work submitted. The Stockport War Memorial Art Gallery team has done a fantastic job hanging the exhibition and it looks visually stunning. Over 140 works are on display and there is a real eclectic mix of paintings, photography and sculpture on display."

Fig 148: 'Ron with Painting Apron', a portrait by Peter Davis of fellow MAFA member Ron Coleman (2018).

The SAG Annual General Meeting of 2017 saw Christopher Rose-Innes, Angela Herd Hall and Ken Anderson continue as President, Chairman and Treasurer respectively. Stephen Johnson, however, stepped down as Deputy Chairman and Peter Holt and Emma Clarke also resigned from the Council. Three members joined the Counil that year: Jason Walker, Peter Davis and Pat Fox-Leonard, alongside existing Council members, Phil Hughes, Linda Lowe, Janet Foy and Mike Heath.

That year, the Guild received a £1,000 donation from Linda Hartley-Rose, in memory of her husband Michael who had passed away the year before. After discussions amongst the Guild Council and the gallery, it was agreed that the money was to be used as a prize fund to encourage young artists, aged between 17 and 25, to enter the Stockport Open. And so the 'Michael Hartley-Rose Award' was born. One hundred pounds and membership of Stockport Art Guild was to be awarded as an annual Stockport Open prize for the next decade.

In 2017, Christopher Rose-Innes and Stephen Johnson, along with external judge Charles Hickson, adjudicated the Guild's 97th Annual Exhibition. There were 142 pieces on show including an oil sketch by Bert Yates; a figurative oil painting by Phil Hughes and two social realist acrylics by Peter Davis. Prizewinners that year included Ron Coleman in the Abstract category; Marlis Pantall in Landscape; Inari Johnson for the Wildlife/Animal category; Susan Coleman in 3D for her Stoneware pot and Lindi Kirwin who received the Colourfield Gallery Award.

One of the Guild's new members in 2017, Neve Ellis, won the Figurative category prize and comments on how she felt at the time:

> *"It probably meant more to me than I could express. Since I got my degree in Games Design I've not been able to work due to illness, so I had no idea how to go forward with my art. Getting my art into an exhibition for the first time, as well as winning a prize, felt like validation, like maybe I could do this for a living some day."*

The Guild Chairman, Angela Herd Hall, adds:

> *"One of the joys for me to see members like Neve come on – you can see it's in her to paint."*

Neve Ellis

Neve Ellis, a 28-year-old self-taught painter from Poynton, joined Stockport Art Guild in 2017. She has a 2:1 degree in Game Art and Design so, as well as traditional drawing and painting, her skills include 2D digital art and 3D modelling. She adds:

> *"I'm also interested in animation and life drawing is recommended for that as well, to study gesture as well as anatomy."*

Fig 149: Life drawing sketch by Neve Ellis (2018).

It was life drawing that drew Ellis to the Guild. She looked on the Internet for ongoing life drawing sessions and SAG popped up in her search results. She recalls from her very first session that she liked the Guild's relaxed atmosphere:

"You can get up and rinse your water mid-session and nobody cares. And if someone's phone goes off or something, you don't get sharp stares like you might at a library.

"I suffer a lot with self-confidence in my art so it helps that I have the Art Guild sessions to go to because it's a planned set time and place specifically for art - there's no putting it off, no 'I'll do it later', art is what you're there to do, and somehow that takes some of the fear away.

I read somewhere that starting a painting is the hardest part, and when the clock hits seven and the session starts, the brush hits the paper, so one of the toughest obstacles is out of the way already."

Fig 150: Neve Ellis with her 2017 prize-winning painting.

Stockport. Change Here

By the start of 2018, there was a renewed sense of positivity about the art scene in Stockport. The War Memorial Gallery was going from strength to strength; the Open Exhibition was back up and running and the Stockport Art Guild, with over 115 active members, was on the rise again too.

Stockport Metropolitan Borough Council launched a campaign in January called 'Stockport. Change Here' about their vision for the future and creating a town that everyone would be proud of. SMBC also began working with Arts Council England with a view to improving the cultural life and opportunities within the Borough. On the 26th January 2018, a roundtable workshop, chaired by Peter Ashworth, took place at the War Memorial Gallery that brought together people from the town's arts and culture sectors to discuss a number of creative opportunities. Angela Herd Hall and Peter Davis represented Stockport Art Guild. This was an exciting time for Stockport and the newfound sense of optimism was starting to be felt everywhere.

The Guild had a busy programme of activity throughout 2018 with regular demonstrations and workshops run by visiting artists including a Portrait Painting demonstration in January by Stephen Ashurst; a series of tutored sessions by John Harrison on urban sketching and a set of three workshops with Ali Hargreaves on 'Still Life with a difference.'

The mainstay of SAG's activites, their portrait and life drawing evenings at the War Memorial Gallery, continued unabated. Current President, Christopher Rose-Innes, now aged 92, still feels as passionately about these sessions as when he joined over thirty years ago:

> *"The reason I joined the Guild was the opportunity to go to the life and portrait evening sessions, but then you find yourself drawn into a kind of community. And in some indefinable way I would miss it very very much and I'm very frightened of the day when I can't drive and it's going to be very difficult for me to get there."*

For the majority of traditional artists, drawing from, and understanding, the human figure is fundamental as a practice. It can help train the eye to see accurately and aid the development of your visual language, compositional skills and spatial awareness. Abstract expressionist, Ron Coleman, believes in the power of life drawing and adds:

"I think the Guild's portrait and life drawing classes are really important for all artists - there's nothing better than working from life. Be it a portrait or life sitting. I think it's good that you've got a time limit and knowing you got to produce something in an hour or whatever – that brings its own enjoyment and fun."

Some members attend SAG's portrait and life drawing sessions to improve their ability to draw people. While art goes through various trends, drawing the human form will always capture our imagination. However, Chairman Angela Herd Hall believes it's not only for the ability to draw people that you should consider life drawing, as it also improves your general drawing and painting skills:

"Nowadays, as a group of artists, I think the standard at the Guild is high. It's pretty accomplished even for people for whom it's not the main thing they do. I say to people don't come with the idea of getting a finished piece of work, just come and enjoy it and it'll show in your work."

Having the sessions based at the Stockport War Memorial Gallery has proved a big motivation for many of the Guild's members. Peter Davis recalls the feeling when he stepped into the gallery for the first time back in 2015:

"The idea of life drawing in a place that's all about celebrating art felt like an honour. Producing work in a public art gallery, with the thought that maybe your work might grace the same walls that have shown paintings by Lowry and Rutherford has definitely helped drive my artistic ambitions. For me, it still feels like a privilege to draw in such an historic building."

Guild Vice-Chairman, Pat Fox-Leonard, builds on Davis's sentiments:

> *"I believe the key principles for the use of the War Memorial Art Gallery continue to this day - the building is still used for the promotion of the best that the borough has to offer in terms of talent and potential. Art exhibitions continue, and poetry is written and read, book launches are hosted, and, on Monday and Thursday nights and some Saturday mornings, anyone interested in mark-making can come to Stockport Art Guild Sessions and carry on the tradition of Remembrance in this iconic building."*

As Stockport Art Guild begins its centenary year, it is now starting to feel like Stockport could become one of the most inclusively creative towns in the area in which to live, work and play. And it has every right to stake this claim with its musical legacy of Strawberry Studios, 10cc and Blossoms; its artistic heritage thanks to LS Lowry, Helen Clapcott and Alan Lowndes who have made the town's iconic viaduct famous through paint and the growing digital and creative tech scene with brands like musicMagpie and CDL now based in the town. Maybe this is the time to pick up the gauntlet laid down 100 years ago by the group's Arts and Crafts forefathers? To echo a four-line stanza from Tony Walsh's poem 'This is the Place' about our neighbouring City, Manchester:

> *And we've got this as the place where a team with a dream*
> *Can get funding and something to help with their scheme*
> *Because this is the place that understands your grand plans*
> *We don't do No Can Do, we just stress Yes We Can!*

Afterword

During the past hundred years, the interaction between Stockport's Art Guild and Manchester's Academy of Fine Arts has played a key role in the artistic journeys of many Guild members, from Harry Rutherford, James Chettle, John Howard and Mary McNicoll Wroe, in the earlier years of the Guild, to Ron Coleman, Angela Herd Hall, Bert Yates and myself from the current membership.

It will be interesting to see how both societies evolve over the coming decades and how the connections continue with the next generation of artists.

Angela Herd Hall, talking about her artistic journey and what the Guild means to her, says:

"If you cut me in half I'd have Stockport Art Guild written through the core. Just by going there every week and doing it I've quietly gained knowledge. I am a product of the Guild and I owe where I am now to the Guild. It's given me the opportunity to draw and paint. I've come up by doing it and here I am. You don't know til you look back just what you've learned."

Piecing together all the information to write this book has been a fantastic, if not challenging, journey of discovery. The journey has not just been about investigating Stockport Art Guild as an organisation, but also its influential artists and all the other members that have contributed to its life and that have made the society what it is today.

To reiterate what John Howard wrote for the Guild's 50th Anniversary Exhibition Catalogue in 1969 when he said:

> *"It must be rare when starting off an organization of our kind, for those responsible to imagine that historical details might be of any interest to those who follow on. It is more likely that immediate problems could seem sufficient burden. Such appears to have been probable with the Guild, so that available historical items are mainly attributable to individual memory rather than official record."*

Fig 151: Peter Davis (left) with Dave Foster (right), grandson of Walter Foster.

Unlike John Howard's peers, I urge every Guild Council member going forward to take heed of his words and document all our stories and events for future generations to discover. That will make the job of the author of the 200th anniversary book a lot easier! It is with this in mind that the Guild has created the role of Archivist and which I, the author of this work, have currently agreed to adopt.

Shaping the Future

As the Guild enters our second hundred years it is important that we look to our history for inspiration, but also to ensure that we do not to live too much in the shadow of our past. We need to move with the times, to reflect the current zeitgeist and to take advantage of any new technology or media that become available. But we also must respect the Guild's history and traditions and the work of all our past members. We may move away from the more elitist attitude of the past but we must always retain our utter respect for artistic ability, effort and integrity without being judgemental about the subject matter, media or motivation. The shape of the Guild's future lies in the artistic hands of all its members and I would encourage us all to be fresh, inquisitive and open to embracing all and any influences that present themselves.

Technological advances are continually shaping the future of artistic creation and providing us with new ways to express ourselves and our thinking about what art can be. In the past, the Impressionists benefitted from new technology such as the invention of portable paint tubes that meant that they could paint en plein air. Andy Warhol arguably wouldn't have become so prolific and so famous without the development of silkscreen printing technology.

Over the past decade, art and digital technology have become more interconnected than ever before. This has revealed new creative horizons beyond the static pictorial and craft sections that have been the traditional fare of the Stockport Art Guild.

I hope that, at some point in the Guild's future, interactive digital installations and Virtual Reality artwork will be seen in the Annual Exhibition just as regularly as an oil sketch or a screenprint are today.

None of us can accurately predict what the future of visual art will look like, the world is changing too fast, and the possibilities of tomorrow are bound to exceed anything we could ever attempt to imagine today. The one thing I am certain about, however, is that, whatever happens, we must continue to put ART into Stockport.

Peter Davis MAFA
Archivist, Stockport Art Guild, 2019

List of Stockport Art Guild members 2019

Correct at time of printing

Ken Anderson
Rose Atyeo
Agnes Barlow
Georgia Bates
Grace Baynham
Andrew Bell
June Bevan
Annette Bonelle
Joan Bradley
Marguarita Bradshaw
Debbie Brophy
Annie Brown
Carrie-Anne Brown
Christine Bull
Joseph Canning
Phillipa Carrington
Pauline Chorlton
Emma Clarke
Ron Coleman
Susan Colman
Damien Cooney

Siobhan Cooper
Doris Cornthwaite
Penny Crinson
Emma Culham
Robin Davies
Peter Davis
Ian Dawber
Gordon Deacon
Lauren Dineen
Mauro Di-Vito
Carol Dronsfield
John Dronsfield
Jena Elliott
Robert Elliott
Neve Ellis
Karl Elphick
Pat Evans
Pat Fox-Leonard
Janet Foy
Chloe Frith
Christine Garner

Madison Gee
Dave Gibson
Lawrence Gottlieb
Christine Grimshaw
Angela Herd Hall
Pauline Hammonds
Ali Hargreaves
Sarah Harris
Mike Heath
Janet Higgins
Clare Hirsch
David Hockin
Phil Hughes
Inari Johnson
Stephen Johnson
Viv Johnson
Maureen Kay
Lindi Kirwin
James Lamond
Margaret Lloyd
Olga Lomax

Linda Lowe
Camilla Luff
Jean Lynch
Susan Markall
Aggie Matyjaszek
Peter McCaldon
Eugene McDonnell
Linda Mealing
Sarah Morley
Thomas Muldoon
Jenny Murdoch
Tilly Murdoch
Ron Murphy
Paddy O'Donnell
Beverley O'Donoghue
Peter Oldham
Myra Oliver
Marlis Pantall
Alan Parry
Katie Patel
John Pegg

Mike Pendleton
Lilian Petty
Stephen Player
Phil Portus
Jeanette Preece
Maggie Preston
S. Judith Pullen
Phillip Purdy
Patrick Ralph
Felicity Ratcliffe
Barbara Redman
Colin Reynolds
John C Riley
Sarah Riley
Neil Robinson
Christina Romero-Vacas
Janet Romero-Vacas
Christopher Rose-Innes
Chloe Rutter
Jennifer Samuel-Bryan
John Sculley

Helen Segar
John Stephenson
Dorothy Thornley
Patricia Turner
Sheila Vaughan
Michael Waddilove
Jason Walker
Heather Warburton
Katie Ware
Gill Warnes
Jean Watson
V M (Feya) Wenham-Bullock
Harry Whittaker
Chris Wilson
Joan Wilson
Pauline Wiltshire
Karen Wise
Bert Yates
Angus Yeaman

List of Images

All images © their respective owners

Fig 1: Walter Foster, self-portrait (circa 1908). Inaugural President of the Stockport Guild of Arts & Crafts. Image courtesy of the Foster family.
Page 8 and 16

Fig 2: Hugh Wallis's design for the 12th year of the Northern Artworkers Guild. Image courtesy of MAFA.
Page 10

Fig 3: 'The Old Grammar School' on Greek Street – view from Wellington Road (circa 1910). Image courtesy of Stockport Heritage Services.
Page 12

Fig 4: The Greek Street School in May 1921, shortly before the site was cleared to make way for the War Memorial building. Image courtesy of Stockport Heritage Services.
Page 13

Fig 5: The fundraising appeal, launched by the War Memorial Committee in December 1919. Image courtesy of Stockport Heritage Services.
Page 14

Fig 6: Watercolour of Beckfoot near Bingley by Walter Foster (1919). Image courtesy of the Foster family.
Page 17

Fig 7: 'SSA 1924' Copper Tray made by Hugh Wallis for Walter Foster. Image courtesy of the Foster family.
Page 18

Fig 8: Detail of Copper Tray made by Hugh Wallis for Walter Foster. Image courtesy of the Foster family
Page 18

Fig 9: Crowd for the 1925 opening of the War Memorial building. Image courtesy of Stockport Heritage Services.
Page 19 and 33

Acknowledgements

This book owes its existence to many people. I would especially like to thank the following individuals (in alphabetical order):

Ken Anderson

Peter Ashworth

Nick Baker

Janny Baxter

June Bevan

Annette Bonelle

Joan Bradley

Andrew Carr

Alf Churchouse

Geoff Clout

Ron Coleman

Natalie Davis

Sheila Dewsbury

Carole Dronsfield

John Dronsfield

Patricia Edwards

Jane Ellis

Neve Ellis

Richard Fletcher

Dave Foster

Patricia Fox-Leonard

Christine Garner

John Hadfield

Mike Heath

Stuart Helm

Angela Herd Hall

Phil Hughes

Ian Irwin

Alexander Leese

Camilla Luff

David Morris

Jeremy Parrett

Ed Perry

Patrick Ralph

Janet Rigby

Neil Robinson

Christopher Rose-Innes

Katherine Rosati

John Saunders

Benedict Sayers

Kate Turner

Jason Walker

Pauline Wiltshire

Bert Yates

Select Bibliography

Alexeev, Vlad.
https://im-possible.info/english/art/pencil/harry-turner.html

Artist Biographies Ltd.
https://www.artbiogs.co.uk/1/artists/northing-clarence-willie

Baharini Baines, Emily Anne. Thesis:
"Design and the Formation of Taste in the British Printed Calico Industry 1919 to 1940" Published by De Montfort University, 2002

Brill, Barbara.
"Pin-up and criticism evening at Stockport Art Guild", Stockport Advertiser, 15th August 1968.

Change.org.
https://www.change.org/p/stop-the-closure-of-stockport-art-gallery-and-war-memorial-during-the-week

Cheshire Life.
http://www.cheshirelife.co.uk/out-about/stockport-sculptor-john-blakeley-reflects-on-his-long-career-1-1644735

Chirnside, John. '
Training of Textile Designers', Published by the Journal of the Textile Institute in 1938

Chiswick Auctions.
https://chiswickauctions.co.uk/brush-sickert-harry-rutherford/

County Express,
"Mr Yates' Red Period", 1960

Daily Telegraph,
L.S. Lowry article, 12th November 1973

Dewsbury,
Sheila.The Story So Far: The Manchester Academy of Fine Arts from 1859 to 2003.

Manchester
The Academy, 2003.

Eden Project.
https://www.edenproject.com/eden-story/our-ethos/manchester-peace-park-kosovo

Fielder, Martin.
"Harry Rutherford," Unpublished biography by Tameside Local Studies and Archives Centre, 2006.

George Bell & Sons.
Walter Crane: "Of the Arts ad Crafts Movement", Ideals In Art: Papers Theoretical Practical Critical. Published in 1905.

Gerry.
https://gerryco23.wordpress.com/tag/harry-rutherford/

Helm, Stuart.
Archivist, Stockport Grammar School

Hemingway, Richard.
"The craftsmen – so different from those paint-sloshers", Stockport Express, 1st December 1966.

Honiton Fine Arts.
http://www.honitonfinearts.co.uk/artists/marjorie-mort/

Hughes, Margaret.
"Plans for 60 more years of art," Stockport Advertiser, 5th July 1979

Hulme, Charlie.
www.davenportstation.org.uk

Hyde Reporter,
The Artist and his Portrait", 1929

Ives, Lawrence A.
"Mr Lowry", The Glossop Chronicle 5th March 1976

Manchester Art Gallery.
J.P. Chettle Memorial Exhibition catalogue, September 1945

Manchester City News,
"Art in everyday life – Mr J.P. Chettle on the Municipality's responsibility" 24th January 1934

Manchester City News,
"Local artist in Stockport exhibition", 26th November 1938

Manchester City News,
"Well known artist's farewell", 6th September 1938

Manchester Confidential.
http://old.manchesterconfidential.co.uk/Culture/Arts/The-lesser-famous-Barry-White

Manchester Evening News,
"500 more jobs axed and gallery opening slashed in town hall cuts," September 2012.

Manchester Evening News.
https://www.manchestereveningnews.co.uk/news/greater-manchester-news/what-happened-stockport-plane-crash-13117279

Martin, Sandra.
"Mr Lowry at home" ISBN 0-901673-32-3

Morris, Josh.
https://www.youtube.com/watch?v=haj3JvR1Upw&feature=youtu.be - North West News, Preston Jan 2014

Noszlopy, George and Waterhouse, Fiona.
"Public Sculpture of Staffordshire and the Black Country." Liverpool University Press 2005.

Rohde, Shelley. L.S. Lowry, a biography.
Salford, Lowry Press, 1999.

Russell, John.
"An Art School That Also Taught Life", The New York Times, 19th March 1989.

Shaw, Stephen.
http://shawweb.myzen.co.uk/stephen/cwnorthing.htm

Stockport Advertiser and Manchester Guardian:
"Two Art Exhibitions at Stockport", 26th September 1949

Stockport Advertiser,
"Annual Exhibition of the Stockport Guild", 7th December 1922

Stockport Advertiser,
"Art Guild creates record", 28th Nov 1974

Stockport Advertiser,
"Judge Leigh Opens Exhibition" 25th November 1938

Stockport Advertiser,
"Local Scenes in Art Guild Exhibition", 12th October 1945

Stockport Advertiser,
"Mr J.P. Chettle", 3rd February 1939

Stockport Advertiser,
"Stockport Guild's Annual Exhibition", 29th November 1923

Stockport Advertiser:
"Self portrait picture for town", 1st November 1979

Stockport Advertiser:
"Art Guild's biggest exhibition draws the crowds", 1st November 1962

Stockport Advertiser:
"Painting is stolen", 20th January 1977

Stockport Advertiser:
3rd November 1927 "Guild of Arts and Crafts Exhibition"

Stockport Art Gallery.
'Fragile State: Art From Kosova' 2007 Exhibition Catalogue

Stockport Express,
"A Painter of merit" 28th December 1944

Stockport Express,
"An Interesting Exhibition, 3rd November 1932

Stockport Express,
"Art Guild's 26th Exhibition", 11th October 1945

Stockport Express,
"Arts and Crafts Exhibition at the War Memorial Gallery" 22nd November 1934

Stockport Express,
"Interesting Exhibition In The Memorial Art Gallery, 20th November 1930

Stockport Express,
"Local Art at War Memorial" 24th November 1938

Stockport Express,
"Stockport Guild's Record Exhibition", 23rd November 1933

Stockport Express,
"Town is aware of art but is apathetic" November 1952

Stockport Express:
"Not the sort of show to pull in the crowds", 11th November 1966

Stockport Grammar School.
http://stockportgrammar-heritage.daisy.websds.net/default.aspx

Stockport Independent,
"Art Guild Exhibition get Gallery Showcase", November 2010

Tameside, Metropolitan Borough Council.
https://www.tameside.gov.uk/museumsgalleries/rutherford/about

Tameside, Metropolitan Borough Council.
https://www.tameside.gov.uk/blueplaque/harryrutherford

The Manchester Guardian,
"Exhibition at Stockport - Arts and Crafts Guild", 19th November 1934

The Manchester Guardian,
"Painters from Stockport" 26th March 1956

The Manchester Guardian,
"Stockport Art Guild – Members Exhibition", 29th September 1937

The Manchester Guardian,
"Stockport Art Guild Exhibition" November 1938

The Manchester Guardian,
"Stockport Art Guild", 12th December 1949

The Manchester Guardian,
"Stockport Art Guild", 2nd December 1935

The Manchester Guardian,
"Stockport Art Guild", 7th December 1936

The Manchester Guardian,
"Stockport Art Guild", 8th October 1946

The Manchester Guardian,
"Stockport Guild of Arts and Crafts", 20th November 1933

The Manchester Guardian,
"Stockport Guild of Arts", 31st October 1932

The Manchester Guardian,
"Stockport Paintings", 17th November 1930

The Manchester Guardian,
"The Red Rose Blooms", 25th November 1939

The Manchester Guardian,
"Woman Painter's Success" 6th December 1935

The Manchester Guardian:
30th November 1923 "Stockport Arts Guild Exhibition"

The Manchester Guardian:
3rd November 1927 "The Stockport Guild of Arts and Crafts"

The Manchester Guardian:
7th December 1922 "The Stockport Arts Guild Exhibition"

The Stockport Heritage Library
Thompson, Margaret. Hugh Wallis (1871-1943): Artist and Art Metal Worker.
Published by Bushey Museum and Art Gallery. 2005

Turner, Philip.
http://www.htspweb.co.uk/fandf/romart/het/hetobit.htm

Varley, Ben.
The History of Stockport Grammar School

White, Barry.
http://www.barry-white.net/welcome/index.html

Whittle, Stephen.
The Art of Harry Rutherford

Yorkshire Post:
"Art out of the attic" 15th January 2010

Yorkshire Ramblers Club.
http://www.yrc.org.uk/yrcweb/index.php/journal/vols6-11/93-vol11-cat/no39/683-v11n39p389

Index